Insolvency:
A practical legal handbook for managers

Peter G Eales FCIB ACIS

GRESHAM
BOOKS

WOODHEAD
PUBLISHING
LIMITED
IN ASSOCIATION WITH
THE CHARTERED
INSTITUTE OF
BANKERS

Published by Gresham Books, an imprint of Woodhead Publishing Ltd, Abington Hall, Abington, Cambridge CB1 6AH, England

First published 1996

British Library Cataloguing in Publication Data
A catalogue record for this book is available from the British Library.

ISBN 1 85573 246 7

Designed by Andrew Jones (text) and the ColourStudio (jacket).
Typeset by Paragon Typesetters, Newton-le-Willows, Merseyside.
Printed by Galliard (Printers) Ltd, Great Yarmouth, England.

Contents

PART IV: CORPORATE INSOLVENCY

17 Corporate winding up: Further provisions 182

Preface

Problems in many areas of insolvency in both the corporate and private sectors of the economy continue to beset us. Even although the latest figures published concerning the appointments of administrative receivers and administrators have declined from the highs of 1991 and 1992, the numbers of such orders and indeed those for full scale bankruptcies and liquidations are still too high. The commercial and private fall-out from this state of affairs is seen to affect more people and businesses as time goes on and there is a growing need for caution and a wider understanding of the intricacies of insolvency law and the diverse ways such rules affect individual circumstances.

A further important consideration must be that insolvency law has changed radically in recent years. Indeed, this process of change is not yet over. At the time of writing, further initiatives are with the Department of Trade and Industry. This may mean more changes and reforms in the coming years.

This book, which covers the main areas of insolvency law and current practice, is aimed at those in industry and commerce, as well as students, who may be interested in this topic. It is hoped that the manager of a credit department who daily faces an assortment of debts owing to his or her business will find this work helpful in deciding on the best path to take *vis-à-vis* chosen debtors. In addition, students working for qualifications in business-related areas, e.g. The

Chartered Institute of Bankers, the Institute of Credit Management, the several accountancy bodies, the Chartered Institute of Secretaries and Administrators and similar bodies will find this volume of help. Part I provides an overview of the subject while the insolvency of the individual is discussed in Part II. The rules covering partnership are dealt with in Part III and corporate insolvency is covered in Part IV. Whilst relevant sections of the Insolvency Act 1986 and Insolvency Rules 1986 are discussed and quoted (along with other Acts of note) care has been taken to give the reader three basic approaches to each topic: definition, procedure and practical considerations. Clearly, in the case of practical considerations, the opinions expressed are the author's own. Thus, in addition to a list of rules, the various topics surrounding insolvency are defined and practical guidance is offered to assist those who may have to weigh up the pros and cons of any action to be taken.

To assist the reader in an appreciation of the various points covering why the law is as it is (and thus the likely approaches of the courts to it), references are made to the several radical changes in the 1986 legislation. It is hoped these may help to clarify this intricate area of the law and assist those readers who take a more academic approach to this subject.

The book is written to the law as it stood in the summer of 1995. Please note that throughout the text, references to 'the Act' or 'the Rules' refer to the Insolvency Act 1986 and the Insolvency Rules 1986 as appropriate. References made to persons in the masculine apply equally well in the feminine.

Finally, may I express my gratitude and appreciation to friends and colleagues Graham Harman-Baker, David Palfreman, Graham Penn and Nigel Sutton for their assistance and helpful comments.

Peter G Eales

Table of statutes and rules

Table of cases

PART ONE

Overview

CHAPTER ONE

Development of insolvency law and practice

History of insolvency

Both the law and practice of insolvency in the United Kingdom can be said to be complicated by any standards. There are many reasons for this, but before we begin any examination of the law or practice, or indeed the philosophy covering the growth of insolvency law, it may be helpful to point out that bankruptcy as a concept of civil law has been around for many centuries. It is interesting to note that down the ages the social attitudes and values of the times can be seen to be mirrored in the harshness of the bankruptcy rules then current. Even today in some areas of the world bankruptcy is seen as a heinous sin if not a crime. That makes for remedies against the bankrupt which may seem horrifying to some observers.

Interests of the creditor

It is important to appreciate that the emphasis in insolvency law differs from one country to another. This can be seen in the insolvency laws within Europe. In the United Kingdom the real concentration is on the rights of the creditor. Whilst the legal position of the insolvent debtor, the rights of employees of, say, a bankrupt employer or the position of an insolvent trader's suppliers and so on are all covered in one respect or another, it is the interests of the creditor which are, quite rightly, paramount. This must and does take full account of the interests of the insolvent debtor.

Early insolvencies

It all started in ancient Rome. Although Roman civilisation was well advanced by comparison to other neighbouring states at that time, life was harsh. If an unfortunate debtor could not pay his debts he was brought before the courts and sold into slavery. The money raised in this somewhat drastic fashion would be used to pay the creditors, or as many of them as possible. In other words the debtor, who had no assets to cover his business or private liabilities, was 'capitalised' to encash his worth. This was apparently the extent of the thinking of the business philosophers of the day.

Advancing several centuries, it appears that bankruptcy was still an extremely grave matter in the United Kingdom right up until the eighteenth century. The insolvent debtor was obliged to surrender 'self and entire estate' to the (then) Commission of Bankruptcy. Failure to do so meant that a complaint to the Commission by an aggrieved creditor brought a mandatory sentence on the debtor of death by public hanging. Several records exist of this dastardly situation, one of the last being the hanging of a Mr Perrott for insolvency in 1761. The statement of a debtor today 'I shall be hanged if I shall pay', was more correctly stated in those days as 'I shall be hanged if I do not pay'.

The twentieth century

The whole area of bankruptcy law and practice was codified and updated in the legislation of 1914. The main statute of that year, the Bankruptcy Act 1914, brought much common sense and a measure of relief to the unfortunate bankrupt. Even so, by modern standards it was harsh. The 1914 Act served well for many years until the law was again updated in 1986 (a minor amending Act was passed in 1976 and the 1925 Amendment Act ironed out some technical points raised in 1914). Changes brought about by the 1986 Act are covered below but it is worth mentioning that the position of the bankrupt with regard to the assets he can keep has been alleviated. The standard of living of the bankrupt, whose financial affairs are under the strict control of the trustee, may be akin to that of an unemployed person on basic social security subsistence. However, the rules are more humane now. The trauma of having to face a public examination is diminished in that such an examination is no longer routine. In the old days it was not unknown for the debtor to be obliged to attend a hearing and face rigorous cross examination in the waiting room of a hospital in which he was a patient at the time. Such a farce cannot happen today. Insolvency law is now much more socially perceptive and is continually under review. Indeed, at the time of writing some radical changes to the process of corporate insolvency law are being examined.

No doubt a writer of insolvency law in the middle of the twenty-first century will look back on the rigours of the law today with horror. That is progress. However, as with criminal law, a fair balance must always be drawn between the accused and the aggrieved (criminal/ victim and debtor/creditor).

The position today

Private and corporate insolvency law and practice were overhauled by the legislation of 1986. When one considers that the Financial Services Act was also passed in that year it can be said that 1986 was indeed a vintage year for financial legislation.

Reform was long overdue in 1986. It is true that minor changes were recommended by the Cohen Committee in 1945 and these were subsequently included in the Companies Act 1948 (covering corporate winding up). The Jenkins Committee made some useful recommendations in 1962, although these were not implemented. Indeed, the subsequent Insolvency Act 1976 (repealed by the 1986 Act) contained only rather trivial reforms. In 1977 the Secretary of State for Trade and Industry appointed Sir Kenneth Cork (then senior partner in Cork Gully and Co), a brilliant insolvency expert, to review the law in its entirety. The result of the deliberations of the Cork Committee, the 'Insolvency practice report of the review committee. HMSO Cmd 8558. 1982', provided Parliament with a cornucopia of useful ideas to consider.

The Cork Report

The Cork Report generated a white paper, 'A revised framework for insolvency law' in February 1984, which contained an outline of many, but by no means all, of the proposals in the original report. This well written and clear work drew on the experiences of other countries. Thus, the position in South Africa and Australia was reviewed and also the rules of Chapter 11 of the United States Bankruptcy Reform Act of 1978. Out of this arose the concept of the administrator appointed under an administration order to control the affairs of an insolvent company. Indeed some of Chapter 11 is now enforced under the Insolvency Act 1986 and it is possible that further sections of Chapter 11 will be brought into United Kingdom law before long. Nevertheless, much of the Cork Report did not see the light of day and Parliament gave the white paper a rough ride.

The Cork philosophy

It is clear that a radical rethinking of the law took place within the 1986 legislation package. Some salient points may be summarised as follows:

(1) The whole insolvency 'industry' is now professional. The work attached to the insolvency of either the individual or the company, e.g. nominee, supervisor of an arrangement, administrator, liquidator, etc. can only be undertaken by a licensed 'insolvency practitioner' (IP). Before 1986 more or less anyone could undertake this work. Now there is for the first time a stringent set of rules to ensure as far as possible fair and honest standards in the industry.

(2) It is now more evident that the court will be concerned to examine the insolvent debtor's affairs with a view to evaluating such questions as:

- Why did he become insolvent?
- Is there a possibility of fraud?
- Is there a matter of public interest to address?
- What are the chances of the creditors being paid and how long will they have to wait?
- Are there any special matters to consider affecting the debtor's family interests, such as the question of the family home?
- How soon will it be before the debtor can be 'put back on his feet' and discharged from bankruptcy?
- Is there an effective alternative to making an insolvency order which will benefit not only the debtor but also, more importantly, his creditors?

(3) It is now paramount that, if an insolvent debtor cannot pay his debts then his financial affairs must be taken away from him and placed in the hands of an expert – the IP – who is answerable to the court (and, of course, to the creditors).

The IP has a choice of action. He may, for example, restructure the existing business or refinance the arrangements of the debtor in the hope that this will avoid full bankruptcy proceedings and enable the creditors to receive better treatment overall (at least avoiding the cost of a full bankruptcy procedure). It has to be recognised that the IP may well have a limited choice of action in those cases where a significant part of the insolvent debtor's assets are secured in favour of his creditors (or taking the corporate scene where an insolvent company's assets are tied up by, say, a floating charge in favour of its bankers). The general position of the secured creditor in an individual's insolvency or in a company's liquidation is often extremely powerful (see Chapter 15). Alternatively, he will opt for a full bankruptcy and, having realised the debtor's assets, will pay the creditors pro rata in accordance with the many rules of law. To avoid full bankruptcy, the individual voluntary arrangement (IVA) has been conceived to provide this choice. It may be said that the IVA is superior to the old deed of arrangement which is still possible under the Deeds of Arrangement Act 1914 (see Chapter 4).

Recent changes in insolvency law

Some more detailed changes in the Insolvency Act 1986, which overtook the Bankruptcy Act 1914, include:

(1) The abolition of the concept of 'acts of bankruptcy'. This was replaced by a 'statutory demand' system, which is much simpler.

(2) The original two-stage system – the receiving order and then the adjudication order – was replaced by a single-stage procedure, the bankruptcy order.

(3) The principle of automatic discharge was introduced whereby the adjudicated bankrupt will in normal cases receive automatic discharge after three years from the date of the order and in cases of 'summary administration', two years (see page 58). In cases of criminal bankruptcy where the debtor is convicted of serious fraud and in cases where the bankrupt has previously been subject to bankruptcy proceedings, the time scale is different. This is covered in detail in Chapter 6.

(4) The rules covering what the bankrupt may keep, that is not surrender to the trustee, have been alleviated to the advantage of the debtor.

(5) There is now a duty on the trustee to call a final meeting of creditors.

There are of course many other important changes in the 1986 Act, especially with regard to corporate insolvency. These changes will be covered in Part II and Part IV.

Recent ideas not adopted

Some ideas in the Cork Report which were not included in the 1986 legislation may be of interest:

(1) There was the requirement that the *Romalpa* clause in a sale contract (the so called retention of title clause) be registered as a floating charge. This is of course mainly a corporate matter and it has come under close Parliamentary scrutiny. No doubt considerations of administration and cost have precluded this reform from being enacted.

(2) It was suggested in the Cork Report that a special insolvency court be created. This would be a fundamental change in the administration of the law in the United Kingdom. Bearing in mind the unfortunate upsurge in the number of bankruptcies in recent years it may be that this reform should have been brought in with the 1986 legislation.

(3) It had been hoped by many people prior to 1986 that the whole question of preferential claims in a bankruptcy or liquidation would be addressed and changes made. It could be argued that the limits on some preferential claims are out of date in modern business dealings. The preferential claim did in fact receive some amendment in 1986 but, some would argue, not nearly enough. There are those – outside Government circles – who would argue that the preferential claim should be abolished.

(4) A radical proposal in the Cork Report whereby the liquidator of a company should receive 10% of the realisations from a floating charge to fund him to carry out his work more effectively was no doubt met with disdain by many in the City, particularly bankers. Perhaps it was just as well this reform did not become law.

Certainly it may be said that insolvency law took a great leap forward in 1986. Even so, at the time of writing the Department of Trade and Industry (DTI) consultative document 'Company voluntary arrangements and administration orders' proposes radical changes in the corporate insolvency rules.

Current statutes

At the time of writing, statutes covering insolvency (both private and corporate) include those listed below.

The Insolvency Act 1986

The Insolvency Act 1986 is the main insolvency statute now in force. Initially the Cork recommendations produced the Insolvency Act 1985 of which only a few provisions came into force in 1986. It was found that a serious disadvantage to the legal position at the time was that the (then) new Companies Act 1985 contained most of the provisions involving the insolvent company. Thus there were two Acts, both new, in force at once which had to be accessed on any question of corporate winding up. The relevant provisions of the Companies Act 1985 were therefore consolidated with the Insolvency Act 1985 to produce one insolvency code: the Insolvency Act 1986. So, for the first time a major part of insolvency law in the United Kingdom became encapsulated in one statute.

Coupled with the 1986 Act are the Insolvency Rules 1986 (SI 1986 No 1925), which provide a long and complete code of rules and procedures in all areas of insolvency work.

The Company Directors Disqualification Act 1986

The Company Directors Disqualification Act 1986 is an important statute which covers the rules affecting the delinquent director. The Act defines what areas of company law are affected, what a misdemeanour or fraud is, and the consequences of wrongful or fraudulent trading on a director's future business life.

The Deeds of Arrangement Act 1914

The Deeds of Arrangement Act 1914 remains on the statute book. It is true that this Act has little practical relevance in today's business climate, largely because the new IVA route is often seen as being preferable to the old fashioned deed of arrangement. However, the deed of arrangement is still a viable option and is relevant to a consideration of modern insolvency practice. This matter is covered in more detail in Chapter 4.

The Insolvency Act 1994

The Insolvency Act 1994 was passed as a measure of urgency. It covers rules concerning the legal effects on administrators of contracts of employment adopted on or after 15 March 1994 (see also Chapter 13).

The Insolvency (No 2) Act 1994

The Insolvency (No 2) Act 1994 covers the details of changes to the rules concerning certain avoidable transactions met with by a trustee or liquidator in a winding up situation (see also pp. 79–80).

The Insolvent Partnerships Order 1994 (SI 1994 No 2421)

The Insolvent Partnerships Order 1994 is a statutory instrument which replaced that of 1986 in full in December 1994. It provides detailed rules on the winding up of a partnership and the effect on the estates of the partners.

Other relevant sources of law

When complicated questions of insolvency law and practice are being examined it will often be necessary to access parts of other statutes, e.g. the Law of Property Act 1925, the Land Registration Act 1925, the Social Security Pensions Act 1975 or some of the many Statutory Instruments in force. In addition, it may well be that the *obiter dicta* of a recent court decision will be pertinent to the problem in hand. Since much of the statute law is still relatively young and the statutory instruments in this area of law are very detailed, it would appear that there is not as yet a wealth of decided cases which fundamentally affect the insolvency situation. However, the multitude of cases on the periphery of company and insolvency law would very likely lead many company lawyers to believe otherwise. Case law, as always, is paramount to any legal analysis.

Thus it will be seen that there is a complex set of rules covering the whole spectrum of insolvency in England and Wales (the laws and procedures applicable in Scotland are not covered in this text) both in the area of individual and corporate affairs. These rules have grown up over the centuries in line with the gradual sophistication of business methods and the continued development of social awareness and social conscience. Without doubt, this complicated arm of the law will continue to grow and, especially in the area of corporate insolvency, one would expect the European influence to continue to hold sway on developments.

This whole subject of insolvency may be seen in part as being like divorce: there are no winners, only losers. There is never enough cash to go round to satisfy all parties. All one can hope for or expect is that the courts, the court officials, the creditors and, not least, the debtor are able to arrive at an equitable solution which is not only lawful but is also seen to be fair and results in the least hurt to the parties involved.

CHAPTER TWO

Insolvency definitions

Problems of definition

Having examined some of the reasons why the whole concept of insolvency law and practice has grown in the United Kingdom as it has, it is surely useful now to define exactly what insolvency is in both legal and practical terms as it applies to the individual and to the company. If someone discussed the affairs of a colleague and referred to that person as being insolvent, that may be in order if it is the truth. The problem lies in the definition, since the current statute law gives at least two definitions of insolvency which have entirely different meanings. The man in the street may well have yet another, equally plausible, definition to offer. A solicitor in court would be clear as to the legal meaning of the term whereas an accountant may have a slightly different but equally relevant interpretation. The lending banker may have yet another viewpoint.

Once the meaning of insolvency can be agreed upon (in so far as that is possible) it may be fruitful to look at some of the more common ways in which a well meaning member of the public can end up in the parlous state of being bankrupt. It is incorrect – even libellous – to refer to someone as a bankrupt until a bankruptcy order has been made against him. Plenty of people are insolvent but they never in fact become bankrupt. Indeed, one of the purposes of the 1986 Insolvency

Act is to prevent the insolvent debtor from becoming bankrupt by offering alternatives to bankruptcy.

Insolvency: The definition

The 1986 Act states in s. 272 (grounds for debtor's petition):

> ... a debtor's petition may be presented to the court only on the grounds that the debtor is unable to pay his debts.

Whilst this definition may be rather vague, the Act is more explicit where limited companies are concerned. The Act s. 122 gives a list of occasions when the court may make a winding up order against a company including 'the inability of the company to pay its debts'. Section 123 of the Act specifies what such inability means:

> A company is also deemed to be unable to pay its debts if it is proved to the satisfaction of the court that the value of the company's assets is less than the amount of its liabilities, taking into account its contingent and prospective liabilities.

This definition is sometimes known as the 'asset test'. Whilst this example of the asset test applies to the corporate debtor, a similar provision is found in the Act s. 341 (3), which states:

> An individual is insolvent if:
>
> (a) he is unable to pay his debts as they fall due, or
>
> (b) the value of his assets is less than the amount of his liabilities, taking into account his contingent and prospective liabilities.

Further elucidation of this definition is found in s. 89 of the Act, which states that before a company may be wound up by means of a 'members' voluntary winding up', which can only happen if the company is solvent, within the five weeks prior to the commencement of the winding up the directors must file at Companies House a 'declaration of solvency'. This declaration states that the directors have made a full inquiry into the company's affairs and that having done so they have formed the opinion that the company will be able to pay its debts in full, together with interest, within a period not exceeding 12 months from the commencement of the winding up.

Whereas s. 89 of the Act does give some clear indication of time scales (for companies) the general concept of insolvency at law may be seen as being vague. So far as individuals are concerned, ss. 267 *et seq.* of the Act (which will be covered in Chapter 6) set out various rules and procedures, e.g. statutory demand, which seem to indicate that the law requires the creditor to imply that the debtor is insolvent. It is up to the debtor by his actions and words to prove that he is in fact solvent or face the consequences. This approach at least gives the insolvent debtor room to move and may assist in distinguishing between genuine insolvency and short-term cash flow problems.

How then do the definitions assist the insolvent debtor? Taking both individual debtors and corporate debtors together for this purpose, there are two basic questions to be addressed:

(1)   Can the debtor pay his debts as they fall due or shortly thereafter?

(2)   Does the debtor have an excess of liabilities over assets?

The question of definition is perhaps not so crucial in the case of the individual debtor since he will surely advertise his insolvency quite adequately by his actions (or lack of them) in failing to pay or compound his debt on receiving a statutory demand. With a limited company the situation is not nearly so clear cut.

The corporate scene

A company may well have a surplus in its balance sheet, i.e. the book values of assets exceed the book values of liabilities. This would be known as a going concern situation. However, the values of assets on realisation (e.g. properties or debtors) may be considerably less than the balance sheet indicates – the 'gone' concern situation. Apart from this, given that the assets do in fact exceed the liabilities (taking into account the value of issued share capital as a liability, which it is) the definition given in s. 123 of the Act is more far reaching. The words 'taking into account its contingent and prospective liabilities' are surely loaded.

So, if a company has assets which are by their nature 'fixed' and difficult if not impossible to sell at reasonable notice, the figure shown for short-term and trade creditors on the accounts may well not be covered by liquid assets, e.g. stocks, bank balances, short-term deposits, etc. Does this make the company insolvent or does it just have a cash flow problem?

The question of contingent liabilities is even more disturbing. A well managed and fully solvent company may have a genuine surplus on its accounts of, say, £150 000. However, the company needs a performance bond from its bank for, say, £100 000 to support a contract entered into with an overseas buyer. The bank will naturally take a counter indemnity from the company for a similar amount, which liability will be shown in the report attached to the final accounts as a contingent liability. Additionally the company may have guaranteed its associate companies to the extent of, say, £100 000 in the normal course of business to assist the group in obtaining bank facilities. The picture has now changed somewhat. The company may well still have a healthy surplus in its accounts. The general reserve figure stands out like a beacon in the balance sheet but the company patently cannot pay off all its debts (actual or contingent) at once or even in a short time. Admittedly the meaning of 'as they fall due' has to be ascertained. If, in addition, the notes attached to the balance sheet indicated large contingent liabilities current, the picture worsens. Thus, what was no doubt intended as a flexible rule of law to allow corporates maximum space to manage their own affairs in safety now becomes an accounting problem.

The need for caution

One thing that is certain is that the creditor of a company, or indeed an individual, may see insolvency in reality and insolvency in the eyes of the law to be quite different. Thus, investigation is necessary before conclusions are drawn. Furthermore, a company's balance sheet and accounts may be out of date long before a creditor gets his hands on them. The cautious lending bank will of course have the option of calling for lists of creditors and debtors, stock holdings and lists from the order book, etc. on becoming suspicious as to the financial stability of a borrowing corporate customer.

In conclusion, the legal definition of insolvency may be said to be deliberately vague. It should be considered alongside not only the accounting questions pertinent but also the rules covering the petitioning of a debtor, etc. in the Insolvency Act.

PART TWO

Insolvency of the individual

CHAPTER THREE

Causes of insolvency

The road to bankruptcy

Having examined the meaning of 'insolvency' and 'bankruptcy', which, as explained, may have more than one application, it may be useful to consider the possible reasons why an individual ends up bankrupt. How does someone go bankrupt? The question is not now being put in its technical or legal sense. That will be covered in depth in Chapter 5. Logic tells us that if one takes reasonable steps in business, gets good professional business advice and, above all, has more than a fair share of luck, then bankruptcy should not arise. Unfortunately, the combination of points given are often not all present. The following situations could well cause insolvency leading to a downturn in business and the eventual financial collapse of the debtor.

Genuine misfortune

Many causes of genuine misfortune can be identified. A person may have made a bad investment, albeit in good faith. A common theme is 'putting all one's eggs in one basket'. Listening to the advice of a well meaning but ill informed friend (never mind the intricacies of the Financial Services Act 1986) can cause havoc. The unfortunate experience of divorce can on occasion lead to bankruptcy. The straightforward collapse of a business, especially a 'one man band', through a change of market direction, changes in public taste, the collapse of an important supplier or the advent of unwanted competition, etc. may result in insolvency unless good advice is sought and acted upon without delay.

In days gone by, when bankruptcy possibly had more of a social stigma than it has today, the courts recognised the hard luck case by giving the bankrupt a 'certificate of misfortune' on his discharge from bankruptcy. This certificate was often valuable when trying to start up again in business or find another job.

Trading without the benefit of limited liability

The benefit of the veil of incorporation as enunciated in the famous *Salomon* v *Salomon & Co Ltd* (1897) case may be more apparent than real today. There are now many exceptions to the rule whereby the owners/directors of a company may be made to account for the misdemeanours of the company. However, the underlying rule still holds good. The fact is that all the owner of a company stands to lose in the liquidation of the company is his share capital, which may be trivial in amount (unless he has guaranteed the debt). However, a sole trader or a partner in a firm stands to lose everything.

The debtor signs a guarantee over the debt of another (person or company) securing the borrower's debt to the bank

A lending banker quite reasonably may say to a shareholder/director of a company: 'If you want us to have faith in your company to the tune of x thousand pounds then is it not reasonable for us to ask you to guarantee your company to the same extent?' Reticence on the part of the director may well lead the banker to doubt the commitment of the director to service the proposed loan and run the company efficiently. Obviously the collapse of the company would enable the banker to call on the guarantor. The terms of the bank guarantee are harsh. Indeed they have to be to enable the bank to carry on normal business with the customer and protect the bank's interests. On the other hand the bank may well require some more tangible security from the owners/directors of the company. Apart from the possibility of taking a debenture from the company, the most suitable and available security may be a director's guarantee secured by a legal charge in favour of the bank over that director's house. The ramifications if the business fails can be immense, particularly if the domestic property secured is in the joint names of the director's spouse and the director.

There are numerous court decisions, which are now good precedents, covering the manner in which such guarantees are taken by the lending bank. The bank should ensure that the director's spouse is *au fait* with the legal undertaking she is signing when joining the guarantee, which she must do if the collateral security is partly in her name. Nevertheless, this type of situation can be extremely difficult where the spouse pleads misrepresentation or undue influence in an attempt to avoid liability when the guarantee is called on by the bank.

Bad or ineffective management

Incompetence or inefficiency in running a business may often result in the proprietor facing bankruptcy proceedings.

Debt burden/interest rates

The burden of trade debt or of meeting increasing interest rates on such debt may be a crucial factor in contributing to the downfall of a business and the bankruptcy of the owner. This appears to have been a significant factor in business failure during the recession of the early 1990s and it highlights the need for a business to have reasonable cash flow management.

The importance of the guarantee

The consequences to a debtor who has signed a guarantee which, if called on by the borrower's bank, may lead to the debtor's insolvency merit further examination.

The sole guarantee

The debtor happily guarantees his company and gives the bank a legal charge on his house which, let us assume, is in his sole name. There are worrying possibilities.

Firstly, when the bank sees fit to call on the guarantor, who cannot pay since his assets are all tied up either in his business or his house, the bank may as a last resort go for a possession order or sale.

However, perhaps the house has lost so much value that the guarantor has a residual debt, which may lead to bankruptcy.

Secondly, if the house is sold in the sole name of the guarantor what action can the wife, who is living in the house, take? She can and very likely will claim that she has an overriding interest in the house up to the value of contributions she has made to the property both at the time of the purchase and since. The Land Registration Act 1925 70 (1) (g) assumes the property has a registered title. If the property is unregistered in title the upshot is somewhat similar although the legal rules differ (*Caunce* v *Caunce* (1969)).

Thirdly, if the wife succeeds in blocking the sale of the house, the bank may still press for repayment. If bankruptcy ensues, then the position of the guarantor and the wife (and indeed that of any children living in the house) becomes extremely difficult after one year from the date of the insolvency order. The Insolvency Act 1986 s. 336 (5) states that 'the court will assume, unless the circumstances are exceptional, that the interests of the bankrupt's creditors outweigh all other considerations. . .' where such application (by the trustee to sell) is made after the end of the period beginning one year from the time the bankrupt's property vested in the trustee (i.e. on his appointment).

The bank guarantor is caught between the devil and the deep blue sea (or, more accurately, between an irate wife and an equally irate trustee).

The joint guarantee

Contrary to popular belief, where a guarantor signs a bank guarantee, which will be a 'joint and several' guarantee, he will not have a ceiling on his liability of a pro rata proportion of the guaranteed amount. If, say, three persons, one of whom is a potential bankrupt, sign a guarantee for £9000 then all three are liable if called on by the bank for the full amount of £9000. Admittedly the person who pays can recover, if possible, proportionately from the others but that is not always easy. Even if a co-guarantor starts off as being perceived to be wealthy, his personal financial circumstances may change. The whole situation can be very dangerous.

The need for caution

One may well reflect that bankruptcy is a respecter of nobody. The simple acts of giving guarantees, increasing stocks in a boom and diversifying into new activities may well pave the way to fortune or, alternatively, the path to ruin if factors beyond the control of the debtor go against him. This is of course the substance of a recession. One must, it is supposed, speculate to accumulate. However, at all times it must be sensible to have a measure of caution and get good advice before acting. In that way the bankruptcy courts may experience a recession.

Society of Practitioners in Insolvency Report

An interesting report has been produced by the Society of Practitioners in Insolvency (SPI) using data for 1993 as follows:

● Average returns to creditors under the voluntary arrangement procedure run at just over 11% compared to 7% for bankruptcies. However, in the North East of England returns under the bankruptcy procedure bring in an average of 28 pence in the pound.

● Tumbling property values and the negative equity gap in recent years have contributed greatly to the bankruptcy of the self-employed.

● Excessive mortgages and debt guarantees tied to homes have likewise forced many self-employed out of business.

● Rather surprisingly, the percentage of bankrupts among the self-employed rose in 1993 to a figure of 80% from 65% in 1992.

● Management failures give rise to 25% of bankruptcies and cash flow problems to 24%. Loss of market (and dependence on a single product) account for nearly 30%.

● It is commented that perhaps consideration should be given to a basic competence test for people thinking of setting up in business for themselves.

● It seems that much of the criticism levelled at banks for 'pulling the rug' from under failing businesses is unjustified since that cause of insolvency – in so far as it can be fairly measured – seems to account for only 3% of failed businesses.

The conclusion appears to be that the legacy of the recession, i.e. redundancies followed by the setting up of small, one-man businesses (never mind the general extravagant malaise of the late 1980s), has been bankruptcies which were all too predictable.

CHAPTER FOUR

Alternatives to bankruptcy

One important aspect of the philosophy behind the 1986 legislation, which is clear in the Cork Report, was the introduction of measures enabling the insolvent debtor to sort out his financial affairs without being adjudicated bankrupt by the court. A number of benefits may accrue from this welcome innovation since the debtor not only avoids the trauma of bankruptcy but he will also be free from the many technical disabilities of the bankrupt. The debtor is able to continue trading and avoid the costs of a full insolvency procedure. For the same reasons the creditor may expect quicker payment of his debts. However, the alternative routes open to the insolvent debtor are not easy options. His affairs are always controlled by a professional IP. Needless to say, any lack of co-operation or misfeasance on the debtor's part may mean his full bankruptcy.

Current options available to the insolvent debtor

There are currently two alternative means whereby the insolvent debtor can avoid an insolvency order being made against him. Prior to a court hearing on a petition for bankruptcy the debtor can opt for:

● a deed of arrangement with his creditors;

or

● an IVA with his creditors.

The deed of arrangement possibility has been with us since 1914 whereas the IVA route was introduced by the Insolvency Act 1986. There are many points of legal and practical interest concerning both these methods of avoidance. It may be best to consider each possibility in turn.

The deed of arrangement

Definition

The Deeds of Arrangement Act 1914 defines the deed of arrangement (DOA) in s. (1) as follows:

(1) A deed of arrangement to which this Act applies shall include any instrument of the classes hereinafter mentioned whether under seal or not:

(a) made by, for or in respect of the affairs of a debtor for the benefit of his creditors generally;

(b) made by, for or in respect of the affairs of a debtor who was insolvent at the date of the execution of the instrument for the benefit of any three or more of his creditors otherwise than in pursuance of the law for the time being in force relating to bankruptcy.

(2) The classes of instrument referred to are:

(a) an assignment of property;

(b) a deed or agreement for a composition;

and in cases where creditors of the debtor obtain control over his property or business

(c) a deed of inspectorship entered into for the purpose of carrying on or winding up a business;

(d) a letter of licence authorising the debtor or any other person to manage, carry on, realise or dispose of a business with a view to the payment of debts; and

(e) any agreement or instrument entered into for the purpose of carrying on or winding up the debtor's business, or authorising the debtor or any other person to manage, carry on, realise or dispose of the debtor's business with a view to the payment of his debts.

In short, the DOA is a contractual arrangement by deed between the debtor and his creditors providing for a settlement or part settlement of his debts.

The definition of the DOA given in the Deeds of Arrangement Act takes into account various types of rearrangement of the debtor's affairs, which can be categorised into two basic methods:

(1) An assignment of the whole (or part) of the debtor's property for the benefit of all his creditors.

(2) A composition whereby the debtor agrees to pay his creditors by instalments from earnings (through the trustee).

The distinction between the assignment and the composition was made clear in the decision *Re Griffith* (1886) as follows:

> Where a debtor makes over his assets to be administered by a trustee, that is a scheme (by way of assignment), where the debtor keeps his assets and undertakes to pay over to the creditors a certain sum, that is a composition.

Thus the composition is not secured. The effect of the composition is that the creditors accept less than the full amount of the debt owing to them by regular instalments. However, the payments may on occasion be covered by guarantors, if any are found.

The deed can encapsulate a combination of the assignment and composition and in order to give it more teeth the guarantee of others, e.g. family members, can be annexed to it. Although no court proceedings are involved in the execution of a deed, the Deeds of Arrangement Act (some 30 sections in all) gives detailed provisions surrounding the formalities of the deed including rules covering registration of the deed and the duties of the trustee.

Procedure

Procedure under the DOA is as follows:

(1) The debtor obtains the consent of an IP (whose title is defined in Chapter 5) to act as trustee and advise on the structure and content of the proposed deed.

(2) The deed is drawn up. The contents will cover *inter alia*:

- parties to the deed;
- rights and duties of the parties involved;
- trustee's fees;
- order of priority of payment to creditors.

(3) A creditors' meeting is not mandatory, although it would seem that, unless there are exceptional circumstances, such a meeting would be appropriate in pursuing point (5) below.

(4) The deed must be registered with the Registrar of Bills of Sale within seven days of the deed having been executed (i.e. signed and dated) by the debtor or any creditor.

(5) The deed must then have the assent of a majority in number and value of creditors within 21 days of registration. The court is empowered to extend this time limit in appropriate circumstances. Claims of creditors for £10 and under are counted for value only. Secured creditors shall be counted in the voting only with regard to any value in their claims after the value of their security has been deducted therefrom.

(6) One of the duties of the trustee is to send to all creditors who have assented to the deed, an updated set of accounts once every six months showing the progress in the scheme.

Practical considerations

It must be said that the DOA is rarely used these days. There are two main reasons why this is so:

(1) Non-assenting creditors can still force through bankruptcy on the debtor.

(2) The DOA has largely been overtaken by the IVA option offered by the Insolvency Act 1986.

The fundamental problem with the DOA is that it does not bind any non-assenting creditors. However, the IVA, once approved by the requisite majority of creditors, binds all creditors of the insolvent's estate. The significance of this point is crucial to all creditors who are approached to consider one of the above routes.

However, provided a debtor can obtain the assent of a majority of his creditors to a DOA this may provide valuable evidence enabling him to defeat a petition for bankruptcy in court by an aggrieved creditor by pleading s. 271 (3) of the Act which states:

> The court may dismiss the petition [for an insolvency order] if it is satisfied that the debtor is able to pay all his debts [i.e. perhaps the petition was 'malicious'] or is satisified:

(a) that the debtor has made an offer to secure or compound for a debt in respect of which the petition is presented [i.e. the petitioning creditor is included in the schedule to the DOA];

(b) that the acceptance of that offer would have required the dismissal of the petition; and

(c) that the offer has been unreasonably refused.

Some may say that the debtor pleading s. 271 has a lot of persuading to do.

Position of preferential creditors

Another problem for the debtor is the fact that it is not a prerequisite that a DOA should give preferential creditors any priority. The deed may do so but it is not mandatory under the Deeds of Arrangement Act. The practical effect here is that a preferential creditor, e.g. HM Customs & Excise, is not likely to assent to a deed unless the VAT element of the list of debts is given priority over the 'ordinary' debts at least to the extent laid down in the Insolvency Act 1986 (see Chapter 8).

Against that, if there are substantial preferential debts in the list then maybe the ordinary creditors would not approve the deed since they would lose what otherwise would be the advantage of a DOA over full bankruptcy.

Each type of creditor will need to examine the nature of his debt alongside the details of the debtor's estate and determine whether a DOA, IVA or a full bankruptcy is the most advantageous course for him, the creditor, to favour.

Further problems

Additional problems associated with the DOA include the following:

(1) If any creditors have reason to believe that the debtor has hidden away any assets or otherwise misbehaved by reason of having conducted transactions as 'preferences' or 'transactions at undervalue', then the DOA will not be acceptable to them. The trustee under a DOA does not have the powers to rectify such transactions in the same way as a trustee in bankruptcy.

(2) The biggest hurdle for the debtor anxious to have a DOA is probably the matter of obtaining the consent of all creditors. Whereas the majority of creditors necessary to assent to the DOA is laid down in the Act (as stated above) the fact remains that all creditors must indicate their reaction for or against the DOA for the purpose of arriving at the required majority figure. This may not be easy.

If a non-assenting creditor to a DOA did successfully petition the debtor in bankruptcy, serious problems would automatically follow. The trustee in bankruptcy could only recover any assets assigned to the trustee under the DOA by attacking the DOA as a transaction at undervalue or a voidable preference (see Chapter 7 for a fuller explanation of these terms). It is questionable whether the trustee in bankruptcy would succeed. This situation could lead to two trustees being interested in the debtor's estate.

However, it is not all doom and gloom with the DOA. This route does have the merit that the court is not involved. If a debtor wishes to keep his financial collapse as private as possible and all his creditors are trustworthy and sympathetic to him, the publicity and trauma of a court action is avoided. Thus, perhaps a DOA is a viable way out of the mess in some cases. A few debtors do still take this option and return to financial respectability through the medium of the DOA.

The individual voluntary arrangement

Definition

Whereas the complex rules covering the IVA are in ss. 252–263 of the Act and the Insolvency Rules 1986 numbers 5.1–5.30, no definition of an IVA is given. A general understanding of the nature of the IVA can be gained from considering the life of such an arrangement. In brief, an IVA may be considered to be a voluntary agreement, which is sanctioned by the court, entered into between the debtor and his creditors whereby the debtor's liabilities are settled by composition or scheme (or by a combination of both, see page 27 above). Similarities can be seen between the DOA and the IVA, although the voluntary arrangement may apply not only to individuals but also to companies. There are other differences. A principal difference is that the IVA is 'court driven' and binds all creditors. One major element of the Cork Report was that deserving creditors be given assurance in settling their affairs without the rigours of full bankruptcy.

If the IVA is solely to be a scheme then the debtor makes over his assets to an IP (the supervisor). A composition involves the debtor keeping his assets – or some of them – and paying his debts out of earnings, asset sales and monies received from third parties, etc. The creditors agree to accept less than full repayment of their debts.

Procedure

Approach a nominee

The debtor, who may in this instance already be an undischarged bankrupt who wishes to have an early release and to settle his debts on a voluntary basis, approaches an IP to obtain his agreement to assist in setting up the IVA. The IP at this stage is known as the nominee.

The debtor and nominee work together and compile the debtor's proposals which will be submitted to the court for approval. The proposals must include the debtor's reasons for wishing to go the IVA route, details of all assets and liabilities now outstanding, the proposed duration of the arrangement and how creditors are to be paid and any other pertinent information.

Interim order

The debtor and nominee go to court with the proposals. The court may now make an interim order whereby for the next 14 days (or a longer period as the court may exceptionally allow) the estate is frozen. Thus, no bankruptcy petition may be dealt with and no other proceedings against the debtor or his property may continue unless the court agrees. It should be pointed out that the court will only make an interim order if it is satisfied that the debtor intends to make a proposal to his creditors and that on the day of making the application the debtor is either an undischarged bankrupt or is in a position to present his own petition (i.e. he is insolvent). Further, the IVA proposals should take account of the rights of secured and preferential creditors unless they agree otherwise.

Nominee's report

The nominee reports to the court within two days before the end of the interim order period. He gives the court viable proposals, the debtor's statement of affairs (unless this has been done when the debtor was made bankrupt, if such is the case) and his, the nominee's, opinion as to the viability of the whole IVA. In particular he must state whether a meeting of creditors is essential.

Creditors' meeting

At this stage the court may extend the interim order as appropriate. The creditors' meeting is then (usually) held to consider the debtor's proposals. The meeting is held not less than 14 days and not more than 28 days after the court considers the report. Creditors have 14 days' notice of the meeting and they may vote at the meeting by proxy. The nominee acts as chairman. The creditors may accept the proposals by voting in favour with a majority in excess of 75% in value of those present and voting in person or by proxy. Additionally the resolution must be approved by at least 50% in value of all creditors to whom notice of the meeting was sent. If the proposals are not accepted by the meeting, the chairman will adjourn the meeting and report accordingly to the court.

It should be borne in mind that the creditors may not accept the proposals of the debtor as they stand. However, provided the debtor agrees to modifications to the scheme put by the creditors, the modified scheme can be taken back to court by the nominee for approval.

The IVA is put into force

Finally, if the court approves the IVA, then any interim order in force will be discharged and, if the debtor is an undischarged bankrupt, steps are taken by the court to have the bankruptcy order lifted. Moreover, by virtue of s. 260 of the Act the IVA, once blessed by the court, binds every person who, in accordance with the rules, had notice of and was entitled to vote at the meeting as if he were a party to the arrangement. Section 260(3) of the Act states 'The Deeds of Arrangement Act 1914 does not apply to the approved Voluntary Arrangement'.

Once the IVA is in force the nominee becomes known as the supervisor. He is of course answerable to the court and supervises in the interests of the creditors the resolution of the debtor's liabilities within the terms of the arrangement. Should the debtor not co-operate with the supervisor and/or step out of line then the supervisor is certain to have the debtor adjudicated bankrupt without delay. More often, with the best will in the world the IVA, despite the initial good intentions and optimism of the nominee and the debtor, simply does not work out. Sadly, in these circumstances bankruptcy is the only option left for the debtor.

Smaller bankruptcies

One further important point arises from the provisions of ss. 273 and 274 of the Act which highlight the general philosophy of current insolvency law. This is that it is now the intention that whenever possible the insolvent debtor should be given the chance to go the IVA route. Also, with the smaller bankruptcies the costs of full bankruptcy can be prohibitive. Accordingly s. 273 provides that where liabilities of the insolvent debtor do not exceed the small bankruptcy level (currently £20 000 unsecured), the debtor has assets worth at least the minimum amount (currently £2000) and the debtor has not been made bankrupt or entered into a scheme or composition or IVA with his creditors for at least five years past, then the court will not grant a bankruptcy petition. Instead an order will be made for an IP to investigate the debtor's position and report back to court with his opinion as to the viability of the debtor entering into an IVA with his creditors.

Practical considerations

The IVA may be seen by some as a fast and comfortable route for the insolvent debtor to alleviate his financial problems. Close examination of the rules, procedures and recent practical experience of IVAs shows that this is not necessarily so. Clearly the IVA is preferable to the DOA as recent statistics of usage show all too well. However, the insolvent debtor should consider whether the IVA route is the best one for him to follow before he rushes into the receiver's office to petition himself. He should also consider the possible pitfalls inherent in this type of financial bail out before signing any papers.

Advantages

The advantages of an IVA may be summarised as follows:

(1) An IVA is certainly less traumatic than bankruptcy and may avoid some of the personal worries of bankruptcy. The IVA route should also be cheaper to administer than bankruptcy. The trustee's fees, which come first in order of payout from the estate in a bankruptcy, can be considerable.

(2) Whilst the debtor must act within the terms of the agreement behind the IVA and remains answerable to the supervisor, he does not suffer the statutory disabilities of the bankrupt. This may mean that he is able to generate an income much more easily than if he had been adjudicated bankrupt.

(3) The debtor has professional help and advice from the supervisor. This could in itself be a source of considerable comfort especially if the debtor has excellent 'technical' skills but finds the administration of the business a problem.

(4) An interim order of the court at the outset of the action may give the debtor a vital breathing space to get his thoughts together and seek advice from his nominee and take a good look – maybe for the first time – at the state of his finances, the effect on his creditors and how best to put his affairs in order. The interim order is certainly not a financial holiday but it provides valuable time – however short – to sort things out.

(5) Once the IVA is approved by the creditors and subsequently by the court the debtor is still not out of danger. However, he is now on the road to recovery and with luck, hard work and patience he should emerge from the situation unblemished.

(6) The IVA route, if it gets through the court system, binds all creditors. This avoids a major difficulty experienced with the DOA, where the approval (or disapproval) of all creditors is mandatory before the deed can be activated.

Disadvantages

The disadvantages of an IVA are:

(1) The debtor must clearly understand that the IVA is not in any sense the end of the road. If he breaks the agreement or tries to hide assets or withhold information or give false information to the nominee/supervisor then he, the debtor, will surely face bankruptcy. The bankruptcy court may be seen here to constitute a 'debtor's hospital'. However, it is a cardinal rule not to upset the surgeon.

(2) As already mentioned, the creditors may in some cases be preferential. This may not be a problem if their status is honoured within the scheme, although problems can arise here *vis-à-vis* the remaining creditors.

(3) If the debtor has, or is thought to have, made recent dispositions from his estate by way of 'preferences' or 'transactions at undervalue' then it is highly unlikely that the creditors will agree to an IVA. The simple reason for this is that such dispositions can only be recovered for the benefit of the creditors generally by a trustee in bankruptcy.

(4) It may transpire that creditors emerge after the creditors' meeting and are thus not bound by the decisions made by the meeting since they had no notice of it in the first place. Such creditors could still proceed against the debtor and, if they are large enough, bring about the downfall of the IVA.

Fortunately, creditors can still obtain VAT relief if they agree to their debts being covered by an IVA (or indeed a DOA). This has not always been the case.

The IP's viewpoint

The IP, who is approached to be a nominee under an IVA, will have to evaluate the position before preparing a viable proposition to put to the creditors and, later, the court. Not least in order of importance will be his evaluation of the debtor. The IP will have to be sure that the debtor is reliable and truthful and that he has not concealed anything and whether the debtor is genuine in his desire to 'come clean' with his creditors. One point of importance will be whether or not there is a business worth preserving, particularly if the interests of employees, suppliers and, not least, the debtor's family are deserving. The debtor will clearly wish to retain some personal assets. Indeed, under the terms of the Insolvency Act 1986 the trustee has discretion (within limits) to allow a bankrupt to retain certain personal possessions. (see Chapter 7). Thus, is the debtor honest and fair in his requirements in this respect?

Lastly, it sometimes transpires that a sympathetic relative or friend is prepared to help the debtor, which may change the picture somewhat in the debtor's favour.

At the very least it can be said that an insolvent debtor should seriously consider the IVA route before either petitioning himself in bankruptcy or letting matters progress to the point when a creditor puts in his own petition.

CHAPTER FIVE

Insolvency of the individual: Preliminary considerations

Bankruptcy proceedings

The whole process of bankruptcy is detailed in the respective sections of the Insolvency Act 1986 and the Insolvency Rules 1986. Whilst the procedure is clearly defined in law, it is complex. Creditors who wish to consider action against a difficult debtor are advised to consider the numerous options and rules involved.

In this chapter the bankruptcy procedure of the individual will be considered while questions surrounding the insolvent partnership and the insolvent company will be covered later in Part III and Part IV respectively.

Bankruptcy proceedings against an individual are inherently of a collective nature. Thus, the interests of all creditors are taken together, although of course the various classes of creditor, e.g. the preferential or the ordinary creditor, are taken separately in correct order of priority. Then again, the position of secured (or partly secured) creditors is subject to specific rules. Thus the petitioning creditor in an individual insolvency is not enhanced as such. The petitioner merely starts the ball rolling.

It is true to say that the whole insolvency process, complicated though it may be, is somewhat simpler than it was under the old rules of the Bankruptcy Act 1914. One example is that the concept of the 'act of bankruptcy' has been removed and thus the initiation of insolvency proceedings against a debtor is simplified. In addition, the rules covering the individual and the company are more in line with each other. Furthermore, the degree of trauma to the bankrupt is slightly less than it used to be. The individual bankruptcy proceedings are now more private. The petition against a debtor is not publicised in the *London Gazette* (although of course the order, if it is made, must be). In addition, the whole question of the public examination has now been reformed in that such proceedings are rare and certainly no longer mandatory. Examinations of the debtor could be vicious and distressing for the debtor without any real reward to the public in terms of pertinent information. Indeed, little but harm often came from them (see page 51).

Who can be subject to bankruptcy proceedings?

Any person with full contractual capacity can be subject to a bankruptcy petition provided that he or she comes within s. 265 of the Act which provides:

(1) A bankruptcy petition shall not be presented to the court under section 264 (1) (a) or (b) unless the debtor

(a) is domiciled in England and Wales;

(b) is personally present in England and Wales on the day on which the petition is presented; or

(c) at any time in the period of three years ending with that day
(i) has been ordinarily resident, or has had a place of residence in England and Wales, or
(ii) has carried on business in England and Wales.

Domicile and residence

The question of residence can be open to interpretation. In *Plummer v IRC* (1987) it was decided that a taxpayer with a house in England as well as one in Guernsey was unable to show that she had lost her English domicile of origin. With regard to the parameter of 'the carrying on of business,' s. 265 (2) of the Act defines this as the 'carrying on of business by a firm or partnership of which the individual is a member'. In addition, the definition widens to the 'carrying on of business by an agent or manager for the individual or for such a firm of partnership'. Moreover, s. 436 of the Act defines 'business' in such a way that it 'includes a trade or profession'. The above definition would seem to be clear and all-embracing. Aliens have to fulfil either the residence or business activity qualification. The position of a creditor in the United Kingdom initiating insolvency proceedings against an alien, who may well qualify under the business category for insolvency action in England, should be considered carefully before proceedings are commenced. In particular, questions arise as to what extent the debtor's assets are situated in England and Wales. If proceedings have to be commenced later in a foreign jurisdiction costly delays may well occur. The rules of international law (in particular, jurisdiction and choice of law) may well apply. However, such matters are outside the range of this work.

Exceptions to the rule

There are exceptions to the class of persons who can be bankrupted through the normal channels.

Minors

Persons under 18 years of age have limited contractual capacities. These are referred to in the Minors Contracts Act 1987. In brief, minors can only be bankrupted in respect of debts incurred on contracts for 'necessaries', e.g. food, clothing, etc. or on judgment debts arising from proceedings in tort or liabilities arising in statute, such as tax arrears.

Persons of unsound mind

Whilst persons of unsound mind can indeed be made bankrupt, action is subject to the control of the Court of Protection.

Deceased persons

No bankruptcy proceedings are possible against deceased persons. However, where a person dies insolvent an administration order may be made against that person's estate for winding up to be made in accordance with the rules of bankruptcy. The administration order overrides the terms of any will left by the deceased.

Which court has jurisdiction to hear bankruptcy petitions?

The Insolvency Rules number 6.9 define the correct jurisdiction applicable to bankruptcy petitions as follows:

(1) The petition shall be presented to the High Court where:

(a) the petition is presented by a Minister of the Crown or a Government Department and is based on an unsatisfied execution or a statutory demand in which it was stated that if a bankruptcy petition was necessary, it should be presented in the High Court;

(b) the debtor has resided or carried on business within the London insolvency district for the greater part of the six months immediately preceding the presentation of the petition or for a longer period than in any other insolvency district;

(c) the debtor is not resident in England and Wales;

(d) the petitioner is unable to ascertain the residence of the debtor or his place of business.

(2) In any other case the petition shall be presented to the County Court for the insolvency district in which the debtor has resided or carried on business for the longest period during those six months.

The matter of residence or place of business is paramount. If it transpires that the debtor is already subject to a voluntary arrangement then the court dealing with the IVA must also handle the bankruptcy (see page 30). For clarity's sake all petitions, wherever lodged, must contain sufficient information to establish the correctness of the choice of court. Furthermore, on filing the petition the court arranges registration of it at the Land Registry and the Land Charges Registry.

Once the questions of whether the debtor falls within the rules to qualify for petitioning and which is the correct court for petitioning have been decided, commencement of proceedings may take place.

The insolvency practitioner

Sections 388 *et seq.* of the Act give the rules covering qualification, authorisation and conduct of the IP.

In 1986, for the first time in the United Kingdom the insolvency 'industry' was given professional status. Previously, various persons could act in insolvency matters with no qualifications to indicate their professional worth or standing. Now, strict rules in the Act regulate the many aspects of insolvency with regard to both the individual and corporate body.

Under s. 388, any person who acts as:

a liquidator, provisional liquidator, administrator, or administrative receiver or as a supervisor of a voluntary arrangement in connection with corporate bodies or as a trustee in bankruptcy, interim receiver, trustee under a deed of arrangement, supervisor of a voluntary arrangement or as administrator in bankruptcy of a deceased's estate in connection with an individual's estate

must be a licensed IP. Various professional bodies have been approved under the Act to issue licences to their members providing such members hold practising certificates. The professional bodies are:

- the Chartered Association of Certified Accountants;
- the Insolvency Practitioners' Association;
- the Institute of Chartered Accountants in England and Wales;
- the Institute of Chartered Accountants in Ireland;
- the Institute of Chartered Accountants in Scotland;
- the Law Society;
- the Law Society in Scotland.

In addition, the DTI is enabled to issue licences to persons who are not members of one of the professional bodies listed above. However, it is essential that such persons exhibit to the DTI ample evidence of extensive experience in administering insolvency work and are suitable and fit persons to hold such a licence. Indeed no one who is adjudged bankrupt or who is subject to a disqualification order under the Company Directors Disqualification Act 1986 may be a licensed IP.

One further point is that it is necessary for an IP to have the following fidelity bonds whilst practising:

- £25 000 general cover;
- a specific bond related to the value of assets involved in the work of a specific appointment. Cover here would range from £5000 up to a maximum of £5 000 000 where the IP is involved in, say, winding up a mammoth corporation.

The advent of the IP with professional status can only be to the good of the insolvency scene as a whole.

CHAPTER SIX

The bankruptcy process

The bankruptcy process follows a set pattern. In effect the courts, IPs, creditors and, not least, the insolvent debtor all travel along a well defined route, which is mapped out by the Insolvency Act 1986 and the Insolvency Rules 1986. Other statutes give additional guidance in certain situations, e.g. the Company Directors Disqualification Act 1986.

Stages in bankruptcy

The bankruptcy process is presented in this chapter as a series of logical stages as follows:

- Stage 1: The statutory demand
- Stage 2: The petition
     - by the creditor
     - by the debtor

     The appointment of an interim receiver

- Stage 3: The hearing
- Stage 4: After the hearing when the order is made
    - the appointment of the receiver
    - the statement of affairs
    - the public examination
    - creditors' meetings
    - the creditors' committee
    - proofs of debt and secured creditors
    - appointment of the trustee
- Stage 5: Discharge of the bankrupt

Other topics such as the disabilities of the bankrupt and the manner in which the trustee winds up the estate will be covered in Chapter 7.

Stage 1: The statutory demand

As has been mentioned already, the procedure in insolvency is now simpler than before. However, clearly an aggrieved creditor cannot simply petition whom he likes as a means of exerting pressure on the debtor to pay, albeit that may indeed be tried from time to time. The court will hear the petition dispassionately and may well take a dismal view of malicious attacks on a debtor. The rule clearly establishes a route which the creditor must take and goes as far as possible to ensure fair play for all concerned.

As explained below, a common method whereby it is established that a debtor is indeed insolvent is for a creditor to serve on the debtor a formal written demand for repayment. Such demand must be served as to content and timing within the terms of the Act and the Rules and is known as a 'statutory demand'. An aggrieved creditor cannot petition a debtor without first complying with the vigorous rules involved.

Background to the statutory demand

Whereas the debtor may petition himself in bankruptcy (see page 46), the other route is for a dissatisfied creditor to do so. In this case the creditor has to comply with a number of rules covered in s. 267 of the Act as follows:

(1) A creditor's petition must be in respect of one or more debts owed by the debtor and the petitioning creditor or each of the petitioning creditors must be person(s) to whom the debt or (as the case may be) at least one of the debts is owed.

(2) A creditor's petition may be presented to court in respect of a debt or debts only if at the time the petition is presented:

(a) the amount of the debt or the aggregate amount of the debts is equal to or exceeds the bankruptcy level [currently £750];

(b) the debt or each of the debts is for a liquidated sum payable to the petitioning creditor, or one or more of the petitioning creditors, either immediately or at some certain future time and is unsecured;

(c) the debt, or each of the debts, is a debt which the debtor appears either unable to pay or to have no reasonable prospect of being able to pay; and

(d) there is no outstanding application to set aside a statutory demand served in respect of the debt or any of the debts.

A number of pertinent points arise here, since the rules stated above may appear to be somewhat all-embracing to the petitioning creditor.

(1) A petition may be presented by one creditor provided his debt exceeds the bankruptcy level. However, two or more creditors may join together to petition a debtor on account of debts which together exceed the minimum amount.

(2) The bankruptcy level, which is currently £750, was raised to that amount from £50 (Bankruptcy Act 1914 s. 4) to £200 (Insolvency Act 1976) and then to the current level of £750 by the 1986 legislation. The somewhat draconian increase in 1986 must have taken many debts out of the bankruptcy net, which no doubt alleviated much of the work of the courts. Thus the ultimate threat of the creditor to the debtor ('I shall make you bankrupt if you do not pay') was taken away from all creditors owed less than £750 (unless they joined in with another creditor). The small claims court was the alternative.

(3) The petition can take various forms, e.g.

- based on a debt due but not based on a judgment;
- based on a demand for a debt presently due under a judgment or a court order;
- based on a demand for a debt due at a future time.

Thus the creditor (or creditors) must establish that the debtor is insolvent and thus unable to satisfy the requirements of the creditor(s) in any or all of the cases above.

Should the creditor be partly secured then he may only make statutory demand on the debtor (upon which to ground a petition) for the unsecured portion of the debt provided that amount exceeds £750.

It should be made clear that s. 268 of the Act clarifies s. 267 (quoted above) by confirming that the statutory demand process mentioned does in effect prove the debtor's inability to pay his debts. However, the test of proof of inability to pay extends to the position where 'execution or other process issued in respect of the debt on a judgment or order of any court in favour of the petitioning creditor, or one or more of the petitioning creditors to whom the debt is owed, has been returned unsatisfied in whole or in part'. Clearly a petition may be grounded on an unsatisfied judgment debt without the formality of the statutory demand process.

The statutory demand must contain the many requirements of the Insolvency Rules 1986 and it must be signed by the creditor or someone authorised to do so by him, such as his solicitor.

Service of the statutory demand

The creditor must do everything he can to serve the demand himself on the debtor. If that is not possible then the use of the postal services may be in order although the creditor may have to satisfy the court hearing the petition that the use of the post was justified. The essence of a statutory demand is to give the debtor at least three weeks either to pay the debt or at least to compound it, i.e. make an effective proposal for payment and/or produce some money on account. Failure of the debtor to pay or compound the debt will give the court which hears the petition proof that the debtor is unable to pay his debts.

Within 18 days from the service of the demand – but no later – the debtor may apply to court to have the demand set aside. Such application must be supported by an affidavit which must exhibit a copy of the demand and spell out the grounds on which the debtor is seeking to have the demand nullified. The court may dismiss the debtor's application or fix a venue and arrange a meeting of the relevant parties after seven days' notice of such meeting has expired.

The court may grant the debtor's application if the debtor has made a counter-claim against the creditor (e.g. set-off, or the debt is disputed on 'substantial' grounds), the creditor has adequate security or there are other grounds which the court considers are sufficient to grant the debtor's request. It can be seen that the Insolvency Rules 1986 afford the debtor ample opportunity to meet his liabilities and at least try to arrange some suitable agreement with the creditor(s) in an effort to stave off a petition in bankruptcy.

Stage 2: The petition

Section 264 of the Act lists the persons who may petition an insolvent debtor in bankruptcy as follows:

(a) one of the individual's creditors or jointly by more than one of them;

(b) the individual himself;

(c) the supervisor of, or any person (other than the individual) who is for the time being bound by, a voluntary arrangement proposed by the debtor and approved under Part VIII; or

(d) where a criminal bankruptcy order has been made against the individual, by the Official Petitioner or by any person specified in the order in pursuance of s. 39 (3) of the Powers of Criminal Courts Act 1973.

Once a petition has been lodged at court it may not be withdrawn without the leave of that court.

This chapter is concerned with the first two of the points listed above. Rules concerning the grounds upon which a creditor can petition an insolvent debtor have already been covered. It is now necessary to look at how a petition works.

Creditor's petition

The creditor's petition must conform to the provisions of numbers 6.6 *et seq.* of the Insolvency Rules 1986 both in nature and by procedure.

The petition must give full details of the debtor with regard to his name (and any false names he may have used), address, nature and address of any business carried on by him, etc. The debt(s) on which the petition is based must be clearly identified as to amount and when due. Any interest due must be specified in addition to which the creditor must confirm that statutory demand has been made (including the date and manner of demand) and that such demand has not been complied with and neither is there outstanding any application to have the demand set aside. The petition by the creditor is supported by an affidavit.

Debtor's petition

Section 272 of the Act states that the debtor's petition may only be made on the grounds that he is unable to pay his debts. The petition must be accompanied by the debtor's statement of affairs containing:

(a) such particulars of the debtor's creditors and of his debts and other liabilities and of his assets as may be prescribed; and

(b) any such other information as may be prescribed [which is similar to that given in the creditor's petition].

Service of the petition

Creditor's petition

The sealed petition must be served personally on the debtor. If it is the case that the debtor is evading such service, the court may order a substituted form of service in an appropriate manner. Where a voluntary arrangement is in force the petition must be sent to the supervisor (unless he is also the petitioner). Service of the petition is proved by affidavit (Insolvency Rules number 6.14).

Normally a court will not hear a creditor's petition until at least 14 days have elapsed since it was served. However, where it is evident that the debtor has absconded or his estate is in jeopardy (i.e. the assets are being 'salted away' by the debtor or otherwise are at risk) then the court may expedite the hearing to a date earlier than the 14 days mentioned. If the debtor consents to an earlier hearing then the court may also expedite the hearing.

Debtor's petition

The debtor's petition is lodged at the appropriate court with his statement of affairs, after which the court will hear the petition as soon as possible. One copy of the petition is returned to the debtor with the date and place of the venue for hearing endorsed thereon. Another copy is sent to the official receiver if he is appointed as an interim receiver. A third copy is sent to an IP appointed by the court. Where a voluntary arrangement is in force the supervisor is also advised and he is given at least 14 days' notice of the hearing.

Appointment of an interim receiver

The court is empowered under s. 286 of the Act to appoint an interim receiver at any time after the presentation of the bankruptcy petition and before the making of a bankruptcy order if it is considered necessary for the protection of the debtor's property. The official receiver will be appointed as interim receiver with such powers as the court grants.

Stage 3: The hearing

Before the hearing the debtor must, if he intends to oppose the petition, not later than seven days before the hearing file a notice in court giving his reasons for his objections to a bankruptcy order. He must also send a copy of the notice to the petitioning creditor or his solicitor. Similarly, before the hearing, the creditors who intend to appear at the hearing must give notice to the petitioning creditor of intention to appear in court. This must specify their name and address, their intention to support or oppose the petition and the nature and amount of their debt. This notice must reach the addressee by the afternoon of the day before the hearing. The petitioning creditor then prepares a list of creditors, who have given notice as specified, for the court.

Thus, on the day of the hearing the court has clear knowledge of the debtor's position and the feelings of some or all of the creditors. Formal proceedings at the hearing should in theory be quick and clear since the 'evidence' has to a considerable extent been supplied before the hearing commences.

Options open to the court

At the hearing of a creditor's petition the court has several options open to it as specified in the Act s. 271:

(1) The court may make an immediate bankruptcy order against the debtor. Before doing so the court must be satisfied on the evidence before it that the debt which was payable at the date of the petition or has since become payable has been neither paid, secured nor compounded. Alternatively, where the specified debt is not yet due the court will have to be satisfied that the debtor has no reasonable prospect of being able to pay it.

(2) The court may dismiss the petition if:

● it is satisfied that the debtor can in the event pay all his debts;

● the debtor makes a firm offer to secure or compound the debt on which the petition is based. Furthermore, the acceptance of such offer (had it been made before the hearing) would have caused the petition to be refused;

● an offer made as above has been unreasonably refused.

Creditors who agree to the compounding of their debt(s) indicate that they will be content to accept less than the full amount owing to them.

In determining under the above rules what exactly constitutes a 'reasonable prospect' of the debtor being able to pay, the court will take full note of the debtor's contingent and prospective liabilities.

It appears that this part of the Act gives the court full power to grant an equitable solution to the debtor's problems and, perhaps very importantly, the rules indicate that the court can take note of the actions of any oppressive creditor who sees fit to use the bankruptcy process as an ultimate weapon to obtain repayment of a debt. At the same time the debtor is treated fairly in so far as he has up to the last moment to retrieve his position by making a sensible offer to the creditors if he is in a position to do so. Section 271 (4) of the Act goes a stage further and defines the term 'reasonable'. Rarely does one see a definition of the one word which may be seen as having furnished the legal fraternity with so much lucrative business in other spheres of law. Section 271 (4) states:

> In determining for the purpose of this section what constitutes a reasonable prospect that the debtor will be able to pay a debt when it falls due it is to be assumed [a rare word in a statute] that the prospect given by the facts and other matters known to the creditor at the time he entered into the transaction resulting in the debt was a reasonable prospect.

The bankruptcy order

If the court grants the petition and makes a bankruptcy order against the debtor then the debtor is officially bankrupt and the die is cast.

On making a bankruptcy order the court will see to it that the order is promulgated in the *London Gazette* and a local paper as appropriate. Thus, the bankruptcy is notified to the world. On occasion, if the debtor appeals against the order, the court may delay gazetting, but this is thought to be rare.

An important factor is that the commencement of bankruptcy for an individual is the date of the order (unlike the compulsory winding up of a company, which commences on the date of the petition or, in the case of a voluntary winding up, the date of the resolution to wind up).

The above points regarding date of commencement and notice to the world are extremely important when the question of the position of creditors is concerned. Thus, the bank where the bankrupt has an account must take steps to safeguard its position. The bankrupt customer is severely inhibited as to his ability to enter financial transactions of any kind (see Chapter 7). The estate of the bankrupt now falls under the management of an IP, receiver or trustee as the case may be, and the bankrupt must 'behave himself', i.e. not commit any bankruptcy offences. These points will be considered in depth in Chapter 7 when the question of the winding up of the bankrupt's estate is covered.

Debtor's own petition presented

Court procedure and decision making differ somewhat when the debtor petitions himself. The philosophy of the Insolvency Act 1986 can be seen here in that the court may be in a position, within the terms of s. 273 of the Act, to guide the debtor back to financial health without the need for full bankruptcy procedure. Thus, the court will not make a bankruptcy order if it appears that:

● if a bankruptcy order was to be made the aggregate amount of the unsecured bankruptcy debts would be less than the small bankruptcies' level;

● if a bankruptcy order was made the value of the bankrupt's estate would be more than the minimum amount;

● within the period of five years ending with the presentation the debtor has neither been adjudged bankrupt nor made a composition with his creditors or a scheme of arrangement with them.

In the above circumstances the court will appoint an IP to prepare a report to consider the viability of the debtor entering into a voluntary arrangement with the creditors. These matters have already been covered (see Chapter 4). However, where the insolvent debtor's total unsecured debts are less than the small bankruptcy level but at the same time his assets are less than the minimum amount the possibility of a voluntary arrangement is extremely unlikely. Even so, in these circumstances the court will be bound by s. 275 of the Act and make a summary administration order over the bankrupt's estate.

Summary administration

An order of summary administration is indeed a bankruptcy, although the estate is so small that a quick settlement of the debts is made in so far as this is possible. The official receiver is only obliged to investigate the debtor's affairs if he thinks fit. Moreover, automatic discharge from bankruptcy may be granted from a summary administration after only two years from the date of the order. This aspect of bankruptcy is covered in more detail later (see page 58).

Stage 4: After the hearing when the order is made

After the hearing when the order is made the debtor is a bankrupt and is thus subject to the rigours of the Insolvency Act 1986 and the Insolvency Rules 1986. Various considerations now apply as described below.

Appointment of a receiver

Whereas the appointment of an interim receiver (if made) ceases on the making of the bankruptcy order, between the order date and the appointment of the trustee the official receiver is 'receiver' and has a duty to manage the bankrupt's estate (s. 287 of the Act). The official receiver has wide powers under the Act including the duty to sell or dispose of perishable goods belonging to the bankrupt which are likely to diminish in value if kept. If he is also a 'manager' then he shall in addition be empowered to take such steps as are thought desirable to protect the value of the estate pending the trustee's appointment. The official receiver may apply to court for a 'special manager' to be appointed over the bankrupt's estate under s. 370 of the Act. The special manager will have whatever powers the court gives him to manage the bankrupt's estate or business.

The official receiver does not wind up the bankrupt's estate. That is not his job and he does not have powers to do so. The trustee will, in time, do that. The official receiver (and special manager if appointed) may be seen as caretaker of the estate with a primary aim to preserve the value of the estate until the trustee can proceed to sell the assets and distribute dividends to creditors in due course. However, a considerable amount of work has to be done by all concerned before that stage can be reached. It can be said that, except where a certificate of summary administration has been issued, it is the duty of the official receiver to investigate the conduct and affairs of the bankrupt. The Insolvency Act 1986 makes this clear although, interestingly enough, the official receiver is only bound to report his findings to the court if he thinks fit. However, by the same section the official receiver is duty bound to report his findings to the court where a bankrupt applies to that court for discharge from bankruptcy under s. 280 of the Act.

Statement of affairs

The debtor must submit a statement of affairs to the official receiver within 21 days of the order date (unless of course the statement has already been produced by the debtor who, in petitioning himself, had to attach the statement to his petition). The statement must give a complete and frank list of debts (secured and unsecured), assets and lists of debtors and creditors, etc. The official receiver will provide the correct form to the debtor and instruct him on the correct manner of completion. If the bankrupt is incapable of completing the form he may apply to the official receiver to have someone else do it for him. In addition, the official receiver has powers within s. 288 (3) to release the debtor from obligation to complete the statement of affairs or extend the time during which the form must be prepared.

The official receiver may request the bankrupt to produce the last three years' accounts prior to the petition and the court may demand accounts before that time. Also, the official receiver may require the statement of affairs to be verified by affidavit and in effect demand any further information he feels to be relevant to the bankruptcy.

The official receiver files the statement of affairs in court. The statement is of course extremely important and unfortunate consequences await any bankrupt who produces less than a full and frank report. The official receiver sends an abridged copy of the statement to the creditors and it is at this stage that the creditors learn for perhaps the first time what chances, if any, they have of eventual repayment.

The public examination

The public examination is a formality which is now only undertaken in cases of real need. The hearing is called after the official receiver has applied to court for such an examination, which may be held at any time between the date of the order and the bankrupt's discharge. Alternatively, the official receiver must make an application to court for a public examination on being requested to do so by one of the creditors who has the concurrence of not less than one half in value of the creditors. Thus, it seems clear that such a hearing is only held when the official receiver feels there is a need or the majority of creditors clamour for this procedure.

At the hearing the official receiver, trustee and any creditor who has tendered proof of debt can appear and question the debtor. The creditors can also, with the approval of the court, act through their solicitor or counsel. The debtor is obliged to appear, and if he fails to attend he is guilty of contempt of court. The bankrupt must answer all questions put to him on oath and he is not entitled to refuse to answer on grounds that he may incriminate himself, although the court may adjourn the hearing if criminal proceedings against him have been initiated.

In the majority of cases of insolvency these days the public examination does not take place, although the threat of such proceedings may well encourage the debtor to co-operate more with the official receiver. Not co-operating with the authorities may well have the result that the automatic discharge from bankruptcy is suspended for a time (see page 58). If a hearing is called then it will probably cover a bankruptcy where unusual or extremely serious aspects concerning insolvency arise, e.g. the possibility of fraud or the possibility of the whole bankruptcy being a matter of public concern.

In any event, a public examination of a bankrupt is not a pleasant event. The Act s. 290 covers this aspect of insolvency proceedings.

The creditors' meetings

Once the bankruptcy order has been made, and assuming there is no summary administration, the official receiver must call a meeting as soon as is practicable within 12 weeks of the day the order was made unless in his opinion no meeting is necessary. This rule does not apply where a criminal bankruptcy order has been made.

If the official receiver decides that a meeting is not needed he must within the 12 week period mentioned notify the court and all known creditors of the bankrupt of his decision (s. 293).

However, under s. 294 of the Act the creditors may request a meeting if the official receiver has decided against holding one. The official receiver will be bound to honour the request of not less than one-quarter in value of the creditors.

The first meeting of creditors is convened by giving them 21 days' notice. Attendance at the meeting may be in person or by proxy.

Voting is available to any creditor who has lodged proof of debt. Where a creditor is partially secured he must value his security and deduct such value from his total debt. The resulting unsecured portion of his debt will form the basis of his vote.

The official receiver will normally be chairman of the meeting and voting is decided by a majority in value of votes cast in person or by proxy.

A word of warning to creditors is apposite here. The question of the creditor's security may not be straightforward. If the creditor is holding funds or other assets in trust for the debtor (this may apply in particular where such matters as 'constructive trust' or the *Romalpa* claim may be evident) then voting power of the creditor may be subject to disagreement with the chairman of the meeting.

The agenda for the first meeting of creditors will in the main be restricted to two important matters:

(1) The appointment of a trustee (or joint trustees).

(2) The establishment of a creditors' committee.

The creditors' committee

The creditors' committee may be established at the first meeting of creditors, as stated above. However, it cannot be formed when the official receiver is the trustee.

The committee comprises not less than three and not more than five of the chosen creditors. Moreover it is formed mainly to perform a supervisory role on behalf of all the creditors. The trustee will report to the committee on all matters of interest during the winding up of the bankrupt's estate and in any case not more than once every two months and not less than once every six months as agreed between creditors and the trustee.

The trustee takes the chair at meetings, the first of which must take place within three months of the establishment of the committee. Subsequent meetings are held within 21 days of a request from a member. A quorum at a meeting is two.

The trustee co-operates with the committee and is often a source of considerable information and comfort. However, he shall not respond to frivolous or unreasonable requests for information which would run up high costs for the estate.

The creditors' committee will determine the trustee's remuneration, which may be based on the time involved in performing the work required by the estate or else a fee may be based on a percentage value of assets realised (see Chapter 17).

Proofs of debt and secured creditors

The proof of debt form is used by all creditors who wish to recover their debt (in whole or in part) and the form must be completed by the creditors and forwarded to the official receiver or to the trustee as appropriate. Chapter VIII of the Insolvency Rules gives full details of the procedure.

The content of the proof of debt form is, as one might expect, a complete analysis of the creditor's claim. Such matters as name, address, amount of claim and how and when the debt was incurred are in the nature of a formality. However, further information is required on the form, e.g. whether the claim includes VAT, whether the debt is preferential and particulars of any security held.

Note that 'security' within the context of the proof form is direct security, e.g. property, shares, life policies or cash, etc. held by the creditor whether by way of legal or equitable charge. Third-party security held by way of guarantee of someone connected with the debtor, whether itself secured by the guarantor's assets or not, does not go on the proof form. Standard bank guarantees specifically allow for such cover to be given by the guarantor under the condition that the guarantor will not compete with the creditor (the bank) in the bankruptcy of the debtor. This can be a source of comfort to the bank in the event of the bankruptcy of a customer.

The official receiver (or trustee) may require that the proof of debt form is given by way of affidavit. Nevertheless, under current rules this formality is only followed on occasion. Even so the completion of the proof form requires the utmost care on the part of the creditor.

If a creditor completes and lodges a proof of debt form and the picture changes *vis-à-vis* the creditor and the debtor, e.g. the figures are changed for whatever reason, the creditor may withdraw the proof form or vary the one already lodged with the agreement of the official receiver (or trustee). In the same vein the trustee or indeed any creditor may apply to court if he thinks that any proof has been wrongly admitted or ought to be reduced.

Foreign currency debts are converted into sterling for proof purposes at the official rate of exchange on the date of the order.

It is up to the creditor to decide when to submit a proof of debt form. It should be remembered that not only does the proof form ensure that the creditor is recognised by the trustee and stands to join in any dividend paid to creditors but also that a creditor who wishes to vote at a meeting of creditors must first prove his debt.

The secured creditor must follow the options provided by the Insolvency Rules numbers 4.95–4.99. He can only alter the value of the security he discloses in his proof form with the leave of the trustee or agreement of the court. However, if he is the petitioning creditor or he has already voted at a meeting in respect of the unsecured portion of his debt then he must seek the permission of the court to change the value he gives on his security.

Partly secured creditors

Choices open to a creditor who is partly secured on his debt are as follows:

(1) Realise the security and prove for the unsecured balance.

(2) Value the security in the proof form and prove for the balance.

(3) Surrender the security to the trustee and prove for the whole debt as an unsecured creditor.

Clearly, if the creditor is fully secured he will not prove his debt at all. He simply realises his security, repays his debt from the proceeds and then hands any surplus proceeds from such security to the trustee.

Security value

It is open to the trustee to test the value of the security which is put in the proof form by the creditor. The trustee simply offers cash to the value of the asset quoted in the proof form and takes over the security to realise himself (perhaps at a higher figure, thereby enhancing the value of the estate). Option (3) above may be one which in the normal course of events holds little attraction for the creditor. Apart from any extraneous problems attaching to the property secured, which may make a sale of such a property unattractive to the creditor, there is the remote possibility that the creditor may see the maximisation of his voting power (as an unsecured creditor) as being a matter of overriding importance.

Appointment of the trustee

The trustee may be appointed as follows:

(1) By the first meeting of creditors (where no certificate of summary administration is in force, in which case the official receiver will be the trustee).

(2) By the court (where the insolvency order is made at a time when a voluntary arrangement is in force. The supervisor of that arrangement may be appointed trustee).

(3) By the Secretary of State (where the creditors fail to appoint a trustee the official receiver must decide whether to apply to the Secretary of State for an appointment to be made (ss. 292, 293, 294 and 295)).

The trustee must be a licensed IP (s. 292 (2)).

Trustee's powers and duties

The powers and duties of the trustee are extensive and are detailed in the Insolvency Act 1986 Chapter IV 'Administration by trustee', ss. 305–335. The Act s. 305 (2) summarises the trustee's functions as follows:

> The function of a trustee is to get in, realise and distribute the bankrupt's estate in accordance with the following provisions of this chapter and in carrying out that function and in the management of the bankrupt's estate the trustee is entitled, subject to those provisions, to 'use his own discretion'.

Furthermore, s. 305 (3) states:

> It is the duty of the trustee, if he is not the official receiver
>
> (a) to furnish the official receiver with such information
>
> (b) to produce to the official receiver, and permit inspection by the official receiver of such books, papers, and other records, and
>
> (c) to give the official receiver such other assistance as the official may reasonably require for the purpose of enabling him to carry out his functions in relation to the bankruptcy.

Another vital section of the Act in this connection is s. 306 which states:

> ... the bankrupt's estate shall vest in the trustee immediately on his appointment taking effect or, in the case of the official receiver, on his becoming trustee.

The section of the Act quoted above is the authority by which the trustee is enabled to realise the debtor's assets and carry out his function in winding up the estate. This complex matter is examined in detail in Chapter 8.

Thus not only does the trustee take possession under the authority quoted above of all books, papers, records, etc. of the bankrupt, he also acquires any choses in action which hitherto have belonged to the bankrupt. Incidentally, notice of such 'assignment' of choses in action to the trustee need not be given by the trustee to relevant parties to such assets in order that he, the trustee, protects his priority to whatever choses in action are available in the bankrupt's estate.

Extensive powers are given to the trustee under s. 314 (and other sections) of the Act including the power to:

- sell the bankrupt's property including goodwill and book debts;
- collect the debtor's monies owing to him;
- make contracts;
- sue and be sued;
- employ an agent and exercise any powers of attorney.

Furthermore with the permission of the committee of creditors (if any), or the court, the trustee may:

- carry on the business of the bankrupt;
- bring or defend legal actions relating to the estate;
- sell property of the bankrupt and accept payment at a later date;
- mortgage or pledge any property of the bankrupt;
- submit to arbitration any claims the bankrupt may have;
- make any compromise or arrangement thought necessary with creditors.

The trustee thus has virtually unlimited powers over the bankrupt's estate. Moreover a number of detailed rules are specifically laid down in the Act and the Rules covering the intricacies of procedure the trustee must follow in gathering the bankrupt's estate together and paying off creditors. Such matters are examined in Chapter 8.

Stage 5: Discharge of the bankrupt

The Act ss. 278–282 give the rules covering the discharge of the bankrupt from the bankruptcy order. It is interesting to note that the recommendations of the Cork Report in this regard were accepted in Parliament and useful reforms were thus enacted. Now for the first time there is a system of automatic discharge which is necessarily geared to catering for uncooperative or even criminal bankrupts and those who have simply not conformed to the rules. This may be seen as a much more satisfactory system of controlling the bankrupt population at any one time.

The release rules currently contained in the Insolvency Act are:

(1)   Where a person has been adjudged bankrupt and he has not been previously bankrupt within the last 15 years (including entering into an individual voluntary arrangement) and such person has not been made subject to a criminal bankruptcy order, an automatic discharge may be granted by the court after the expiry of three years from the date of the bankruptcy order.

(2)   Where the bankrupt is subject to a summary administration order then, subject to the same conditions as in (1) above, the release order may be given by the court after only two years from the date of the bankruptcy order.

(3)   Where the debtor has been bankrupt within the last 15 years or he is subject to a criminal bankruptcy order, the bankrupt must apply to court for discharge at an opportune time. However, no such application can be made until the expiration of at least five years from the date of the bankruptcy order.

For undischarged bankrupts who await the right of automatic discharge under (1) and (2) above the word 'automatic' may have a somewhat hollow ring if they have been in any way obstructive towards the receiver, trustee, or indeed any creditors. Any so called bankruptcy offences committed by the bankrupt will certainly count against him. The official receiver has the right under the Act s. 279 to apply to the court for the automatic discharge to be suspended. The court will then require the official receiver to submit a full report giving his reasons. A hearing will be fixed at which the bankrupt may reply and give his version of events.

When a bankrupt is discharged the court will give him a formal certificate of discharge. In addition he can require his discharge to be advertised in the *London Gazette* or in any appropriate local newspaper. On discharge from formal bankruptcy the bankrupt will consider whether the discharge is indeed the end of the matter. Section 281 of the Act clarifies this point. It appears that the release from bankruptcy discharges him from all 'bankruptcy debts' but the release has no effect on:

- the right of any secured creditor to enforce his security;

- any debt of the bankrupt which was secured by means of fraud or fraudulent breach of trust;

- the bankrupt's debts in respect of court fines, damages incurred for negligence, judgment debts or debts under any order by a court in respect of certain family or domestic proceedings.

Under s. 282 of the Act the court has the power to annul a bankruptcy order at any time if the order should not, in the opinion of the court, have been made in the first place. In addition the court may annul a bankruptcy order if it appears that, within the rules, all debts and expenses of the bankruptcy have been paid or secured since the making of the order.

The court may annul a bankruptcy order whether or not the bankrupt has been discharged from bankruptcy. Thus it would appear that if a bankrupt repays all his bankruptcy debts – some even after his discharge – he can, so to speak, have the slate wiped clean.

CHAPTER SEVEN

The status and estate of the bankrupt

An insolvent debtor is not considered at law to have committed a criminal offence merely by reason of being bankrupt: that is unless the debtor is adjudicated under a criminal bankruptcy order or the receiver's or trustee's investigations unearth fraud on the bankrupt's part. Indeed in many insolvency cases a considerable degree of sympathy is often due to the insolvent debtor whose financial condition may have resulted largely from misfortune beyond his control. However, once a bankruptcy order is made against an insolvent debtor the legal status of the adjudicated bankrupt is clear. The Act specifies a number of legal disabilities which attach to the bankrupt. Moreover, the bankrupt is compelled under the terms of the Act to co-operate with the receiver and trustee and certain actions, termed 'bankruptcy offences', if taken by the bankrupt during the period of his adjudication, attract penalties specified in Schedule 10 of the Act. Such penalties involve fines and/or prison sentences. In addition, the Company Directors Disqualification Act 1986 s. 11 covers corporate directors and their personal bankruptcy.

The Insolvency Act 1986 restricts the business abilities of adjudicated bankrupts during the period of the bankruptcy.

Bankruptcy offences

Bankruptcy offences under the Act ss. 350–362 are set out below.

Non-disclosure

The bankrupt must inform the official receiver of all disposals of property before the bankruptcy which in any manner affect the total value of his estate. He must disclose and deliver up all assets of whatever nature and not conceal anything. He is also guilty of an offence if he removes or conceals any property and he cannot give a satisfactory explanation for the loss of his property within the 12 months before the petition.

Concealment or falsification of books

The bankrupt must not hide, destroy or falsify any papers, ledgers, records, etc. in an attempt to conceal the true state of his financial position.

Fraudulent disposal of property

The bankrupt must not make any gift or transfer of property within five years of the presentation of the petition with the intention of defeating the aims of the receiver or trustee.

Absconding

If the bankrupt leaves England or Wales within six months prior to the petition carrying not less than £500 of his property he will be considered to have committed an offence.

Fraudulent dealing with property obtained on credit

It is an offence for the bankrupt to have disposed of goods or property obtained on credit within 12 months of the petition where at the time of disposal such goods had not been paid for in full.

Obtaining credit: Engaging in business

The bankrupt cannot obtain credit alone or jointly with someone else for more than £250 without disclosing his bankrupt status first to the lender. Furthermore, the bankrupt cannot (directly or indirectly) engage in business under any name other than that in which he was adjudicated bankrupt without disclosing to all parties with whom he transacts business that he is indeed bankrupt.

Failure to keep proper books of account

The bankrupt must have kept proper accounts within the two years before the petition and continue to do so if he carries on trading (within the rules and directions of the receiver and/or trustee) thereafter.

Gambling

The bankrupt is guilty of an offence if he has, within a period of two years before the petition, contributed 'materially' to his insolvent position by gambling or, say, hazardous property or share speculation.

Intentions behind the rules

It will be seen that the rules have a theme. Most of the rules are in effect retrospective. The Insolvency Act 1986 is not drafted to catch insolvent debtors who are subsequently adjudicated bankrupt. The Act s. 352 is worth quoting here. It states:

> Where in the case of an offence under any provision of this chapter [i.e. the list of offences related above] it is stated that this section applies, a person is not guilty of the offence if he proves that, at the time of the conduct constituting the offence, he had no intent to defraud or to conceal the state of his affairs.

The essence of the rule is that where the court can be convinced that the bankrupt concealed property or papers innocently or he invested a small amount of money in a property foolishly but without fraudulent intent, he will be excused the action. If, however, he had sold his major assets and bought gold coins, which he concealed (or sent overseas), he will have the full wrath of the court on his head. In any case fraud is punishable quite aside from the bankruptcy aspect of it.

The rules are of course subjective and, whilst proof of an offence may be simple, cases can be envisaged where much discussion and pleading in court by the receiver, the bankrupt and others will take place before a specific position is resolved.

It is probably fair to say that if the bankrupt is honest and truthful he has little to fear from investigation at the hand of the trustee or the court hearings. Once again though the interests of the creditors are paramount.

Company directorships

The Company Directors Disqualification Act 1986 s. 11 states that it is an offence for an undischarged bankrupt to act as a director of, or directly or indirectly to take part in, or be concerned in the promotion, formation or management of a company except with the leave of the court. This definition, which is wider than is generally thought, encapsulates not only the director but also the bankrupt who, having been a director of a company, continues to manage a company with a lesser title. The bankrupt cannot resign his directorship, which he must do, only to carry on his activities with a company under the title of, say, head of the post room. Penalties stated in the Act are severe. Further aspects of this matter will be covered in Part IV.

Disabilities of the bankrupt

The principal disabilities of the adjudicated bankrupt are in the sphere of his business activities and in public life. The rules are:

(1) The bankrupt cannot alone or with another person obtain credit of more than £250 without disclosing his status to the person from whom he obtains his credit (the Act s. 360). Neither can he engage in trade without disclosing his status.

(2) The bankrupt cannot by virtue of the Act s. 427 be elected to vote or sit in the House of Commons or the House of Lords.

(3) Under the Act s. 390 the bankrupt cannot be a licensed IP.

(4) As stated above the bankrupt cannot be a director of a registered company or take part in the management of a company without the leave of court (Company Directors Disqualification Act 1986 s. 11). Moreover, the leave of the court will not be given unless intention to apply for it has been served on the official receiver. If the official receiver feels that such an application by the bankrupt should be refused on the grounds of public policy it is his duty to attend the hearing and oppose the application.

The disabilities of the bankrupt may seem somewhat draconian. Once again it is the interests of the creditors which prevail. However, the financial good of the public at large is taken into account in preventing the bankrupt from causing further problems.

The estate of the bankrupt individual

Present position

The Act went some way to making the involved process of the realisation of the bankrupt's assets and subsequent distribution of proceeds to creditors simpler than it used to be. Thus, the provision of the Bankruptcy Act 1914 s. 37 which covered the principles of 'relation back' have been (almost) abolished. Similarly, the concept of 'reputed ownership', which was never easy to prove, is no longer with us. Many other concepts of the 1914 Act have nevertheless been carried through to the 1986 Act. The rules concerning so called protected transactions (Bankruptcy Act 1914 ss. 45 and 46) are now reborn in the Insolvency Act 1986 s. 284 even though this section has been seen by some as being difficult to interpret and even extremely obscure. However, it is fair to say that the current legislation is a step forward and affords the bankrupt a fairer progress through a difficult time.

The progress made by the trustee in winding up the estate is of vital interest to all creditors and, it is suggested, this process may be of crucial concern to the banker who holds the account(s) of the bankrupt.

The trustee

The responsibility of the trustee is primarily to gather in the assets of the bankrupt before distributions to the creditors are made. The appointment and duties of the trustee have already been covered in Chapter 6, from which it will be seen that the trustee has both heavy responsibilities and extensive powers. It is only the trustee who can in fact realise the bankrupt's assets. His appointment as trustee gives him the necessary authority. However, in practice it is often the case, as has already been discussed, that the trustee is not in fact appointed until some time after the court has made the bankruptcy order. This gives rise to a further set of rules regarding the policing of the estate in this interim period of the winding up.

The distribution process

It may be of help to review the complex sets of rules in the Insolvency Act and the Insolvency Rules in the matter of the winding up of the individual's estate in stages. Vital periods in the bankruptcy process are:

- the period before the petition;
- the period between the petition and the bankruptcy order;
- the period between the order and the appointment of the trustee;
- the period between the appointment of the trustee and the discharge order.

The time between the petition and the discharge order will be considered first, since the time before the petition can be more easily taken as a separate issue. The trustee must of course examine thoroughly all relevant information at his disposal on appointment including the statement of affairs, reports from the official receiver, bank statements, building society statements, share transaction notes, invoices, personal and business ledgers and correspondence, etc. of the bankrupt. Following that the trustee will trawl through the estate and identify any transactions of the bankrupt which have taken place prior to the petition to establish whether any such dealings can be reversed or challenged within the insolvency rules. In this way the trustee 'reconstitutes' the estate in accordance with the rules and maximises the chances of the creditors receiving equitable treatment.

Whilst the trustee will have the advice and wishes of the creditors at creditors' meetings or, more likely, at meetings of the creditors' committee the Act s. 305 clarifies the trustee's general position, e.g.

(1) This chapter [IV] applies in relation to any bankruptcy where

(a) the appointment of a person as trustee of a bankrupt's estate takes effect, or

(b) the official receiver becomes trustee of a bankrupt's estate.

Moreover, as we have already seen:

(2) The function of a trustee is to get in, realise and distribute the bankrupt's estate in accordance with the following provisions of this chapter: and in carrying out that function and in the management of the bankrupt's estate the trustee is entitled, subject to those provisions, to 'use his own discretion'.

And

(3) It is the duty of the trustee, if he is not the official receiver

(a) to furnish the official receiver with such information

(b) to produce to the official receiver and permit inspection by the official receiver of such books, papers, and other records, and

(c) to give the official receiver such other assistance as he [the receiver] may require.

The trustee, if he is not the official receiver, thus has considerable freedom but he is also tied by many rules which require him to co-operate with the authorities.

Before the realisation of the estate within the time scales set down is considered in detail, certain preliminary matters should be addressed.

Property which the bankrupt may keep

The old adage that the bankrupt will 'lose the shirt off his back' is not literally true, although some may say that the position falls little short of that. The Act s. 283 (2) specifies the property which the bankrupt may keep:

(a) such tools, books, vehicles and other items of equipment as are necessary to the bankrupt for use personally by him in employment, business or vocation;

(b) such clothing, bedding, furniture, household equipment and provisions as are necessary for satisfying the basic domestic needs of the bankrupt and his family.

Section 283 (3) states that the above does not apply to:

(a) property held by the bankrupt on trust for any other person, or

(b) the right of nomination to a vacant ecclesiastical benefice.

Assets held by the bankrupt which are subject to charge in favour of a creditor will of course remain so charged. The largest asset of a bankrupt may well be his matrimonial home, which is often registered in the joint names of himself and his spouse. This matter is covered below.

The above list of assets which the bankrupt may keep may seem somewhat vague. At least the monetary limit placed on the value of such assets by the Bankruptcy Act 1914 has been removed. The trustee has, as has been stated, some discretion in the matter within the rules. However, s. 283 of the Act has an interesting limitation imposed on it by s. 308, which states:

Where

(a) the property is excluded by virtue of section 283 (2) ... e.g. tools of trade, household effects etc. from the bankrupt's estate and

(b) it appears to the trustee that the realisable value of the whole or any part of that property exceeds the cost of a reasonable replacement for that property or that part of it, the trustee may by notice in writing claim that property or, as the case may be, that part of it for the bankrupt's estate.

The practical effect of s. 308 is that the bankrupt may not hide behind the effects of s. 283, which is quoted above, to defeat his creditors. Thus, if any insolvent debtor realises he may be facing an adjudication order he may try and be clever and invest what little money he has left in buying an antique four-poster bed. He may be under the illusion that, if he goes bankrupt the bed will be protected. The trustee may well serve the bankrupt at a later date with a s. 308 notice whereupon the bailiffs will take the bed away, sell it, and hand the proceeds to the trustee after a cheap divan bed has first been purchased for the bankrupt's use. In that way the fund for the creditors is adjusted to a more reasonable level.

The matrimonial home

The bankrupt's home always poses a difficult problem. It may well form the bulk of the value of the bankrupt's estate. Innocent parties, that is the bankrupt's wife and children, are also vitally affected as to the court's decision and the timing of any sale of the home. The court and the trustee have to balance the interests of the bankrupt's family and the creditors. There are also further matters to resolve, e.g. whether the property is mortgaged and if so what proportion of the equity is tied up. Is the property registered in the bankrupt's sole name or is it registered in the joint names of himself and his spouse? In addition, where the bankrupt is leasing a property the lease may even contain a bankruptcy clause whereby the lease is forfeit on the adjudication of the lessee, although it is thought that such leases are not in favour these days. Sections 336, 337 and 338 of the Act cover the rules concerning the bankrupt's matrimonial property.

Section 313 of the Act is clear in that where a trustee cannot for any reason realise the matrimonial home on the market he must apply to court for an order imposing a charge on the property for the benefit of the estate. The trustee's application to court must be full and cover the extent of the bankrupt's interest in the property, amounts still owed to creditors and details of the registration of the house, etc. However, the court is bound by the terms of s. 336 of the Act to consider:

- the interests of the creditors;

- the conduct of the spouse or former spouse so far as it contributes to the bankruptcy;

- the needs and financial resources of the spouse or former spouse;

- the needs of any children (under 18 years of age);

- all the circumstances of the case other than the needs of the bankrupt.

Under s. 337 of the Act, even where the bankrupt is living without a spouse the order of court is needed where the bankrupt has living with him a child under 18 years of age.

The bankrupt's spouse will have the right of occupation in the house under the provisions of the Matrimonial Homes Act 1983 provided such right is registered. Nevertheless, even if this is not the case the permission of court is still needed before a sale can take place by the trustee. These provisions of the Act are only designed to give the bankrupt's spouse modest protection. Certainly, no protection is given to co-habitants. Thus, the co-habitee of a bankrupt may be a common-law wife or a relative. The law is the same for each.

The feelings of the creditors will be assessed by the court in line with such matters as: is the house such that it is beyond that considered necessary for the bankrupt's lifestyle? Has the bankrupt contributed to his bankruptcy by buying a house beyond his means? The house may be registered in the joint names of the husband and wife, although in reality the bulk of the cost of the house has been met by the bankrupt – partly at the cost of his creditors. Has the house been mortgaged by the husband and wife to support the husband's failed business venture when the husband should have realised the financial position he was in? All these questions may well be weighed up by the court in detail before a solution which is equitable to all parties is found.

The above provisions may be seen as giving the bankrupt and his spouse a chance to get themselves sorted out. Admittedly in times when property is difficult to sell this chance is not worth much in practical terms. However, s. 337 (6) puts the lid on the matter so to speak and states:

> Where such application [to court for sale] is made after the end of the period of one year beginning with the first vesting of the bankrupt's estate in a trustee [note: not the order date] the court shall assume, unless the circumstances of the case are exceptional, that the interests of the bankrupt's creditors outweigh all other considerations.

The intention of s. 337 (6) seems to be clear enough. After one year from the vesting date the trustee should be able to have a sale order. The section contains words and phrases such as 'assume', 'exceptional' and 'outweigh all other considerations'. It is perhaps just as well that the section does not give the court maximum leverage even at that late hour. However, the intention is there and presumably the bankrupt would need a strong argument to delay a sale of the home after one year. Real hardship would, it seems, have to be pleaded with conviction. Again the interests of the creditors take on special meaning.

Property of the bankrupt which the trustee may disclaim

The trustee may within the provisions of ss. 315 *et seq.* of the Act disclaim any onerous property which forms part of the bankrupt's estate. This is broadly property which is more trouble than it is worth. The Act defines it as:

(a) any unprofitable contract;

(b) any other property comprised in the bankrupt's estate which is unsaleable or not readily saleable, or is such that it may give rise to a liability to pay money or perform any other onerous act.

One can envisage that a trustee may well wish to disclaim an onerous lease which contains draconian lessee's covenants and is thus difficult to sell. Then again, a parcel of partly paid shares in a small company may well be subject to a disclaimer by the trustee.

The trustee must file a notice in court covering all particulars of any part of the bankrupt's estate which he wishes to disclaim. Once the court has noted and returned the disclaimer form to the trustee he must give copies of the notice within the following seven days to all persons who may be affected by it. Any person who suffers loss by such act may prove for that loss in the bankruptcy. The person may also apply to court to claim an interest in such disclaimed property. If the trustee receives a notice requiring him to confirm whether or not he will disclaim an item of the bankrupt's property he must take action within the following 28 days.

Income payments order

The trustee is entitled to secure the receipt by him of a portion of the income of the bankrupt if he is in any doubt as to the efficacy of any direct arrangement he may have with the bankrupt. The trustee can ensure that the bankrupt is not salting away any income he may receive after the adjudication. Even so, the court which receives an application for such an income payments order will look closely at the reasons for such a request.

Regulations covering the income payments order are contained in the Act s. 310 and the Rules numbers 6.189–6.193.

The trustee must make an application to the court for an income payments order which, if granted, will oblige the payment of such income specified in the order to be paid by the bankrupt to the trustee on receipt of the funds or may oblige the payer to remit direct to the trustee. However, the Rules make provision for any such order to be varied or reviewed from time to time. Furthermore, the order will normally be discharged on the bankrupt's discharge from bankruptcy unless the court at the time of release makes the order of discharge from bankruptcy conditional on the continuation of such order for a period up to three years from the date of discharge.

Analysis of the estate

It is now appropriate to examine the bankrupt's estate from the point of view of the trustee. As has been pointed out the trustee will, *inter alia*, be responsible under the terms of the Act and the Rules for maximising the assets of the bankrupt's estate for the benefit of the creditors.

There are many rules covering the various stages in the bankruptcy of the individual. As already mentioned, the stages are:

- the period before the petition;
- the period between the petition and the order;
- the period between the order and the appointment of the trustee (otherwise known as the vesting date, i.e. the date upon which the assets of the bankrupt vest in the trustee);
- the period between the vesting date and the bankrupt's discharge.

The commencement date of the bankruptcy is the date of the order.

The property of the bankrupt (apart from that which remains in his possession) vests in the trustee on his appointment (s. 306 of the Act). Thus, while the trustee cannot touch the estate until he is appointed (which may be some time after the order) the distributable estate is that which exists (or did exist) at the date of the order. This is in effect a ghost of the old doctrine of 'relation back' which was effectively abolished.

A further problem is that, unlike the case with a corporate winding up, the petition in the case of the individual is not advertised in the *London Gazette*. Thus, creditors may not have knowledge of such a petition having been lodged before the hearing date. Indeed the creditors may well not appear at the hearing to consider the petition. Nevertheless there is no guarantee that all creditors will have knowledge of a petition and their first intimation that anything is wrong could well be that they have noticed the order advertised in the *Gazette*.

Certainly this aspect of bankruptcy is of very real concern for banks running current accounts for insolvent customers. The position may be further complicated if there is more than one account for the insolvent customer and any of these accounts shows a credit balance. Apart from the question of the bank's right of set-off (combination of accounts) which is covered later in this chapter, the bank is duty bound to account to the trustee in due course (and prove for any debt which is unsecured if required) with correct figures which pertained at the date of the petition.

The bank account in general

'Dispositions' are transactions entered into by the insolvent debtor which have the effect of diminishing the debtor's estate and thus reducing the assets of the debtor on bankruptcy to the ultimate detriment of the creditors.

Staying with the example of the bank running one or more current accounts, and possibly a loan account for an insolvent customer (although the rules do not concern banks exclusively), the following problems may be encountered:

(1) A payment may be made to the debtor's account at the bank and the bank may wish to set this off against an unchallenged debt. This payment may be attacked later as belonging to the trustee.

(2) The bank may have an unchallenged deposit in the name of the debtor which it wishes to set off against an overdraft. The trustee subsequently may attack the debt as one which should not have occurred.

Thus, the bank may have an overdraft of say £5000 and a deposit of say £2000 in the name of an insolvent debtor. In the normal course of events the bank would have the statutory right to set off the two balances and, in the absence of security lodged by the customer, would prove for the net debt of £3000. The bank would not welcome the trustee attacking the deposit as being out of order and demanding the deposit be paid over to him leaving the bank to prove in the estate for the full £5000. The decision in *National Westminster Bank* v *Halesowen Pressworks & Assemblies Ltd* (1972) highlighted this problem.

The Act s. 284 provides comprehensive guidance with regard to the above situation. Section 284 (1) states:

> Where a person is adjudged bankrupt, any disposition of property made by that person in the period to which this section applies [the period beginning with the day of the presentation of the petition for the bankruptcy order and ending with the vesting date, s. 284 (3)] is void except to the extent that it is or was made with the consent of the court or was subsequently ratified by the court.

This seems clear in that dispositions as stated can only be safe if made with the consent of court or later ratified by the court.

However, it would be unsatisfactory if the position rested there, especially for the bank which may well continue accepting credits for an account or pay cheques, etc. in ignorance of the lodging at court of a bankruptcy petition. Fortunately, s. 284 (4) takes care of this:

> The preceding provisions of this section do not give a remedy against any person:
>
> (a) in respect of any property or payment which he received before the commencement of the bankruptcy in good faith, for value and without notice that the petition had been presented, or
>
> (b) in respect of any interest in property which derives from an interest in respect of which there is, by virtue of this subsection, no remedy.

With regard to the period between the order and the vesting of the estate in the name of the trustee, s. 284 (5) appears to cover this:

> Where after the commencement of his bankruptcy the bankrupt has incurred a debt to a banker or to any other person by reason of the making of a payment which is void under this section, that debt is deemed for the purposes of any of this Group of Parts [i.e. section of the Act] to have been incurred before the commencement of the bankruptcy unless –
>
> (a) the banker or person had notice of the bankruptcy before the debt was incurred, or
>
> (b) it is not reasonably practicable for the amount of the payment to be recovered from the person to whom it was made.

This subsection does state 'banker or person' but it is clearly targeted in the main at bankers.

It is now necessary to examine how these subsections of the Act work in practice. Although the rules in s. 284 may seem obscure to say the least, their practical application can be considered step by step.

First, a consideration of s. 284(1)–(4), which covers the date from which the petition is presented to court until the vesting date. There are four possibilities as to the application of the rules to a running current account, depending on whether the account is overdrawn or in credit (the application to loan accounts is identical).

The account is overdrawn

Credits
The credit is indeed a disposition in favour of the bank. The debtor could have applied the money to, say, the cost of a holiday or put it on a horse. Instead, he chose to give it to the bank in reduction of his overdraft. This is a diminution of his estate. One possible sticking point is that s. 284(4) of the Act demands that the payment is received 'in good faith and for value, and without notice etc.' Whilst the 'good faith' is not questioned, the words 'for value' may be. The bank in collecting the cheque for credit to an overdrawn account has a lien on the cheque by virtue of s. 27(3) of the Bills of Exchange Act 1882. Thus, the bank is deemed to have taken the cheque for value. The cheque is collected before the order date and the question of it being a disposition arises. The bank must prove that it had no notice of the petition or alternatively have the court ratify the transaction if it is to have the protection of s. 284(4). Failing this the bank will be obliged to return the funds to the trustee and prove for the original (larger) debt in the ensuing insolvency of the customer.

Debits
A cheque paid from an overdrawn account would not be a disposition

of the debtor's estate. Indeed it is a disposition of the bank's funds. Providing the cheque is paid before the gazetting of the insolvency order the bank could prove for the debt caused by paying such cheque in the debtor's bankruptcy.

The account is in credit

Credits
There is little in this transaction to concern the banker. He merely pays a larger balance caused by the credit to the trustee in due course. However, where a debit balance in the customer's name also exists, questions of set-off may arise (see Chapter 8).

Debits
This may be the worst scenario to be faced by the banker. Suppose a customer had a credit balance of £5000 and drew a cheque for £2000 on his account before the hearing but after the petition. The balance on the account after the petition would fall to £3000. There would be no remedy against the payee for this money if the payee was unaware of the petition by virtue of s. 284 (4) (b) of the Act. The trustee would demand the return of the £2000 paid away and, in the absence of the court's ratification to the transaction, it would be likely that the bank would have to pay the trustee the full (original) balance of £5000 and be left to prove in the estate for the £2000.

This position may seem to be harsh to the innocent banker, although the court might listen sympathetically to his plea. Often a bank holding a credit balance for an insolvent debtor, against whom a petition in bankruptcy has been lodged, will have had notice of the petition from one source or another.

The bank account after the order

Once the bankruptcy order has been made the bank will be aware of the situation from the notice in the *London Gazette*. Banks know the routine well. Once the order is gazetted the only remedy the bank may have is contained in s. 284 (5) of the Act, which is quoted above. The effect of this subsection appears to be that if the banker had no notice of the gazetting and the payee of the cheque, which the banker has paid, is difficult to approach, then payment may stand to the extent that the debt it represents may be treated as though it had occurred before the order. This would then bring the debt under the rules of the rest of s. 284. This complicated rule appears to be derived from the case of *Re Wigzell* (1921), where a petition was contested and pending appeal the receiving order (a process now defunct) was not advertised. The hardship apparent to the creditor in that case was alleviated by the Bankruptcy (Amendment) Act 1925, since encapsulated in s. 284 of the Act. Maybe if the printers of the *Gazette* were on strike the rule would be invoked. In practice, the disposition after the order is without protection unless the court were to ratify such dealing for extraordinary reasons.

As far as banks are concerned in day-to-day accounting matters the rules indicate that the account of any insolvent customer must be stopped or blocked immediately the bank learns of a petition. Protection at law is available to the innocent banker who is unaware of developments. If a bank misses the gazetting of bankruptcy affairs of a customer or ignores other relevant information, this may well result in the bank losing funds with small chance of recovery in the ensuing bankruptcy of the customer.

The bank account after vesting date

During the period between the appointment of the trustee and the discharge of the bankrupt it is imperative that the bankrupt co-operates in full with the trustee. If the bankrupt acquires or receives any property or if his income increases, he must notify the trustee of all details within 21 days of such occurrence (s. 333). The Rules number 6.200 then states that the bankrupt must not dispose of any such assets for 42 days. During this time the trustee will doubtless take such action as he deems appropriate regarding such property or income. Should the bankrupt dispose of any such asset within the 42 day period referred to without having given statutory notice to the trustee then such 'after acquired' property may be reclaimed by the trustee for the estate. Note that the terms of the Act s. 333 (2) refer to such dealings 'after the commencement of the bankruptcy' (the date of the order) whereas in practice the terms of the Insolvency Rules given above are more likely to impact on the winding up of the estate after the vesting date. Presumably if the bankrupt receives property after the order date and before the vesting date the official receiver will take a keen and immediate interest in the event.

Prior to petition date

Sections 339–349 of the Act under the heading 'Adjustment of prior transactions, etc.' are of special interest to creditors (past and present) and in particular to bankers of the insolvent debtor. The trustee is by no means only concerned with the debtor's estate from the petition date. On the contrary, the financial dealings of the debtor before the petition may well present the trustee with difficult problems which the above quoted sections of the Act seek to clarify. Once again the philosophy of the Act shines through with a simple question: Are the creditors as a group being treated equitably and rateably? Prior creditors, who are now paid off, may be tempted to heave a sigh of relief on learning that a petition is down for hearing after settlement of their particular debt, believing they have been paid just in time. This is not necessarily the case if, as a result, the other creditors have been wrongfully disadvantaged (within the meaning of the Act).

The measures which enable the trustee to trawl through the bankrupt's estate are contained in the sections of the Act quoted above. It is necessary to take each type of 'questionable transaction' which the bankrupt made before the petition in context. It may be of course that in any one particular estate no such transactions occurred. The opposite may well be the case where the bankrupt has been less than honest and was well aware of his impending financial disaster and sought to look after his friends. Creditors such as the Inland Revenue or HM Customs may display much righteous indignation on learning this.

Thus it is necessary to dissect the rules, the reasons for the rules and the practical effects of the rules for each transaction referred to as follows.

The transaction at undervalue

Transactions at undervalue are defined by s. 339 (3) as follows:

(a) he [the bankrupt] makes a gift to that person [the creditor or donee] or he otherwise enters into a transaction with that person on terms that provide for him to receive no consideration;

(b) he enters into a transaction with that person for a consideration of marriage; or

(c) he enters into a transaction with that person for a consideration the value of which, in money or money's worth, is significantly less than the value, in money or money's worth, of the consideration provided by the individual.

The timing of such a transaction is any date within five years before the presentation of the petition against the debtor (s. 341 (1)).

The above occurrences need explanation. In overall terms the philosophy of such rules appears to be that the giving away of an asset by the debtor or the sale of an asset at an absurdly low price (being a sham) has the net result that the estate of the bankrupt, which is subsequently available to creditors, has been reduced by the amount of the undervalue.

The above transaction cannot be fair to the other creditors. It is no good for an insolvent to try and salt away or warehouse his assets with a friend or relative in the hope that if he becomes bankrupt the trustee cannot then utilise the assets in the eventual distribution of the estate to genuine creditors. As s. 339 of the Act points out: 'the court shall, on such an application [by the trustee on discovering an undervalue] make such order as it thinks fit for restoring the position to what it would have been if that individual had not entered into that transaction'. This implies that the recipient of the undervalue must pay to the trustee such amount as constitutes the undervalue (the full value of the gift or the shortfall between the value of the article and the actual price paid) and be left to prove in the estate for such sum as an unsecured creditor. Now the Act s. 341 (2) does make the situation clear in that the bankrupt must have been insolvent, i.e. unable to pay his debts when due, when he made the undervalue or, alternatively, became insolvent as a result of such a payment or gift. However, insolvency by the debtor is presumed unless otherwise shown where the undervalue is in favour of an associate. It may be difficult on occasion for a trustee to prove the insolvency provision where the undervalue is in favour of a non-associate and took place some years before the petition.

An interesting example of the application of s. 339 of the Act occurred during the case *Re Kumar (a bankrupt)* (1993). The facts of this case were as follows:

⬤ The husband transferred half the equity in the matrimonial home owned by himself and his wife by deed dated 11 June 1990 to his wife. The house was then worth £140 000 on which there was an outstanding mortgage of £30 000 which the wife took over in full.

⬤ In January 1991 the couple were divorced on the wife's petition and a consent order was later made in the divorce court which dismissed any claim the wife may have had for capital provision since the husband had already given the wife the bulk of his assets, e.g. half the equity in the matrimonial home.

⬤ Later in 1991 the husband became bankrupt and the trustee claimed to have the transfer of the half share in the house as an undervalue.

The trustee reasoned predictably that the transfer by the husband to his wife of his half share in the house constituted an undervalue within the meaning of s. 339 of the Act. The only consideration provided by the wife to the husband for the transfer was her acceptance of the mortgage liability outstanding amounting to only £30 000. The house was worth £140 000 and thus the wife received a half share in the house considerably in excess of the mortgage liability she was taking over. The transfer was made before the divorce and presumably the consent order was overtaken by events. The trustee was successful in having the transfer set aside as an undervalue.

The question of a debtor entering into a transaction with a person in consideration of marriage being an undervalue is of interest. It is thought that this provision is intended to adjust a somewhat peculiar provision of the old Bankruptcy Act 1914 wherein it provided that marriage contracts were exempt from the undervalue rules. Nowadays an insolvent debtor cannot 'invest' the bulk of his assets in giving his daughter an over-generous provision on her marriage in an effort to defeat his creditors.

The preference

The Act s. 340 (3) defines the preference as follows:

> An individual gives a preference to a person if:
>
> (a) that person is one of the individual's creditors or a surety or a guarantor for any of his debts or other liabilities and
>
> (b) the individual does anything or suffers anything to be done which (in either case) has the effect of putting that person into a position which, in the event of the individual's bankruptcy, will be better than the position he would have been in if that thing had not been done.

Furthermore, the same section of the Act specifies that the individual giving the preference was 'influenced in deciding to give it by a desire' to produce in relation to that person the effect mentioned in (b) above. In addition, by reason of s. 340 (5) of the Act a preference given to an associate by the debtor is presumed to have been influenced by the requisite 'desire' unless the contrary is shown. As in the case of the undervalue it has to be proved that the debtor was insolvent when the preference was made or became insolvent as a result of it.

The court will make an order on being shown that a preference has taken place restoring the position to that shown for the undervalue. Difficulties over the meaning of an application of the preference have occurred for many years. There have been particular problems in this area for banks which have granted overdrafts to customers only to find that the customers have been made bankrupt. An interesting case in this connection is *Re M Kushler Ltd* (1943). Here, a bank quite innocently took assignments over life policies of a director, Mr Kushler, to support his guarantee in favour of the bank over the company's debt. In the event, Mr Kushler withheld payments to other creditors with the intention of repaying the bank as quickly as possible and thus having his guarantee released. This act was compounded by Mr Kushler when he deliberately concealed from his creditors at the first meeting with them that his guarantee to the bank even existed. The Court of Appeal then ruled that the payments into the bank were clearly made in preference to the other creditors with the object of discharging the guarantee and the bank was obliged to refund the monies received to the liquidator. The position of the bank in this type of situation is – or may be – simply that it has to prove as an unsecured creditor in the estate, whereas it started out as a secured lender with a guarantee backed up (in this case) by a life policy. This situation is untenable to a lending bank and the guarantee forms used by banks for guarantors to sign contain clauses covering such situations. For example, the 'security' behind the guarantee can be revived, the guarantee could continue until at least 24 months after the repayment of the debt and the guarantee is the property of the bank and thus not for eventual release to the guarantor.

The timing of the preference is important. Section 341 (1) states that a preference shall subsist for a period of six months before the petition or two years before the petition if the recipient is an associate of the debtor (an associate being the debtor's spouse or relative, or spouse of a relative of the debtor or debtor's spouse).

Recent changes

The Insolvency (No 2) Act 1994 clarifies the position of a person who has received a benefit from someone who has passed on monies, etc. received as a result of a transaction at undervalue or by way of preference. As already stated the court has powers under the Act ss. 339 and 340 to 'make such order as it thinks fit for restoring the position to what it would have been if that individual had not entered into that transaction' (e.g. the undervalue or preference). Section 342 of the Act goes into some detail as to exactly the measure of relief the court may give to the situation and how it is to be given. Section 2 of the Insolvency (No 2) Act 1994 amends s. 342 (2) of the 1986 Act. It is worth recounting the revised s. 342 (2), which now reads:

An order under section 339 (undervalues) or 340 (preferences) may affect the property of, or impose any obligation on, *any person whether or not he is the person with whom the individual in question entered into the transaction or, as the case may be, the person to whom the preference was given* [author's italics throughout]; but such an order:

(a) shall not prejudice any interest in property which was acquired from a person *other than that individual* and was acquired in good faith and for value or prejudice any interest deriving from such an interest, and

(b) shall not require a person who received a benefit from the transaction or preference in good faith and for value to pay a sum to the trustee of the bankrupt's estate, *except where he was a party to the transaction or the payment is to be in respect of a preference given to that person at a time when he was a creditor of that individual.*

The 1994 Act then adds a new subsection, s. 342 (2A), to the 1986 Act as follows:

Where a person has acquired an interest in property from a person other than the individual in question, or has received a benefit from the transaction or preference, and at the time of that acquisition or receipt:

(a) he had notice of the relevant surrounding circumstances and of the relevant proceedings or

(b) he was an associate of, or was connected with, either the individual in question or the person with whom that individual entered into the transaction or to whom that individual gave the preference, then unless the contrary is shown, it shall be presumed for the purposes of paragraph (a) or (as the case may be) paragraph (b) of subsection (2) that the interest was acquired or the benefit was received other than in good faith.

The Insolvency (No 2) Act 1994 then elucidates 'relevant surrounding circumstances' to be the fact that the individual in question entered into the transaction at an undervalue or else the circumstances which amounted to the giving of the preference by the individual in question. Furthermore, the words 'notice of the relevant proceedings' are taken to mean notice of the fact that the petition on which the individual in question is adjudged bankrupt has been presented or of the fact that the individual in question has already been adjudged bankrupt.

It would seem that the purpose of this new legislation is primarily to identify those circumstances where a person who has – albeit indirectly – benefited from a transaction at undervalue or a preference can keep his money. Clearly such receipt of money must be in good faith (i.e. received honestly) and 'for value' (i.e. for consideration and not as a gift). In addition, where it can be shown that the ultimate beneficiary of the monies/value in question:

- has received such monies dishonestly;
- has received them without consideration, i.e. as a gift;
- has notice that the original donor has been petitioned in bankruptcy or else is bankrupt;
- is party to a transaction which in any way forms part of a three-way deal involving the insolvent debtor or bankrupt;

then the court will be enabled to reclaim any or all monies from the current holder and leave that person to claim in the bankrupt's estate as an unsecured creditor.

Doubtless this new provision will plug some loopholes to the benefit of genuine unsecured creditors.

General considerations

The Cork Committee appears to have examined the question of the preference in depth. Two interesting and helpful reforms were made in 1986. First, the Bankruptcy Act 1914 s. 44, which defined the preference (then known as the fraudulent preference), gave rise to the requirement that the debtor had to have the 'dominant intention' to prefer the creditor paid. The Insolvency Act 1986 only requires the debtor to be 'influenced by a desire' to pay the preferred creditor. This distinction is designed to prevent creditors from deliberately pressurising a debtor who is thought to be near insolvency to pay, with the intention of establishing that the debtor had at the time no dominant intention to pay but rather paid through fear of action against him if he did not pay. A recent case, *Re M C Bacon Ltd* (1990), threw light on the meaning of the words 'influenced by a desire'. In this case the bank required security to enable it to continue the existing overdraft facility. The debtor had little choice but to comply if the facility was to be granted. The claim of preference against the bank quite rightly failed.

The second reform brought in by the Act in this area of preference lies in s. 342(1)(e), which provision was not available before 1986. This section states that a court making an order covering a preference may:

provide for any surety or guarantor whose obligations to any person were re-leased or discharged (in whole or in part) under the transaction or by the giving of the preference to be under such new or revived obligations to that person as the court thinks appropriate.

This new provision may be a comfort to banks, especially those caught by the likes of Mr Kushler. As mentioned above, the Insolvency Act 1986 gives the necessary protection to banks (or any other lenders) anyway. Admittedly the section referred to is slightly vague, e.g. the words 'as the court thinks appropriate' may seem loose, but the position of the lender who takes a guarantee appears to be covered.

Extortionate credit transactions

The Act s. 343 defines an extortionate credit transaction as one which:

having regard to the risk accepted by the person providing the credit:

(a) the terms of it are or were such as to require grossly exorbitant payments to be made (whether unconditionally or in certain contingencies) in respect of the pro-vision of credit or

(b) it otherwise grossly contravened ordinary principles of fair dealing.

Furthermore it is to be assumed that a transaction with respect to an application in this context is or was extortionate.

In the case of this type of transaction the time scale is three years before the commencement of bankruptcy (the order), not three years before the petition. The court has extensive powers under s. 343 (4) to order the rectification of the position so that the bankrupt's estate in the hands of the trustee is restored to what it would have been without the transaction.

Neither the trustee nor the undischarged bankrupt may apply under s. 139 (1) (a) of the Consumer Credit Act 1974 for the agreement by which such credit was provided to be reopened.

Once again the trustee has powers to have the value of the estate rectified where it has been dissipated by the bankrupt by his action in entering into absurd credit transactions which he could not afford.

The trustee may well handle an application covering the type of transaction mentioned above as one which constitutes both an extortionate transaction and a transaction at undervalue.

In addition to the above list of recoverable transactions in the hands of the trustee the question of such transactions being tainted with fraud is important. Any transaction – undervalue or not – which 'puts the assets beyond the reach of the person who is making, or at some time may make, a claim against him, or otherwise prejudices the interests of such person in relation to the claim which he is making or may make' (s. 423), is possibly making a transaction tainted with fraud. The court will have wide powers to rectify the matter.

The problem of whether or not the bankrupt is guilty of fraud is a separate issue from bankruptcy as such, although the bankruptcy order may be made as a criminal one. Fraudulent transactions are free of time constraints.

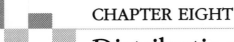

CHAPTER EIGHT

Distribution of the bankrupt's estate

The trustee will research, investigate, collate information and account for the estate and report to the official receiver and creditors. The procedures explained in Chapter 7 will be followed and in time the trustee will be ready to distribute the assets, or those that are left, to the creditors. In this chapter the essential rules and procedures for this part of the individual's bankruptcy will be examined and in particular the position of the creditors.

Creditors

Before the trustee can distribute any funds from the estate to creditors, all creditors must first submit proof of debt claim forms to the trustee. Indeed, the creditor cannot even vote at a meeting unless the proof form is agreed by the trustee. The question of proof of debt and the position of the secured creditor has already been examined (see page 54).

Classes of creditor

Creditors are divided into classes for purposes of priority for pay-out of funds as follows:

- secured creditors;
- preferential creditors;
- ordinary creditors;
- deferred creditors.

All classes of creditor (apart from fully secured creditors) are treated alike. This is according to the principle of *pari passu* which is strictly adhered to by the trustee in all cases, whereby all creditors within a class have the same chance of repayment.

It is necessary to examine the legal status of each class of creditor in turn.

Secured creditors

In practical terms secured creditors do not line up with other creditors when the trustee makes a distribution. The secured creditor has various options open to him which have already been discussed (see Chapter 6). If the secured creditor is still owed money by the bankrupt after he, the creditor, has realised his security and applied the proceeds to the debt, then the creditor must prove for the balance of monies owing as an unsecured creditor.

Preferential creditors

Preferential creditors are in a special position, as the name implies. This will become more apparent later in this chapter when the distribution procedure is covered in full. However, in short, the preferential creditor is privileged in that he receives payment of his debt from the bankrupt estate in full before any ordinary creditor. The concept of the preferential creditor has been established in statute law for many years and the Cork Committee was aware that many sections of the business community had expressed considerable concern at the position of preferential creditors. The final Cork Report took full note of the views which had been given to the committee. Cork recommended that in future the preferential system be cut back to include only those monies which relate to taxes and duties collected by the debtor as agent for the Crown (e.g. PAYE collected from staff pay or VAT monies owing).

The Insolvency Act 1986 produced few real changes to the rules covering the preferential claim despite the advice given in the Cork Report. Perhaps this was to be expected. Only two meaningful changes are noticeable:

(1) Rates and taxes (such as corporation tax) are no longer preferential.

(2) The preferential period for VAT has been reduced from 12 months to 6. The preferential time scales for other taxes and duties such as PAYE, social security contributions and betting duty are still 12 months.

It will be appreciated that the whole concept of the preferential debt applies to both the individual and the corporate bankruptcy. The application of these rules to the company liquidation will be covered later (see Chapter 16).

A complete list of preferential debts is given in Schedule 6 of the Act as follows:

● *Debts due to the Inland Revenue* Amounts deducted from the pay packet of an employee during the 12 months before the order and not paid to the tax authorities.

● *Debts due to Customs and Excise* Any VAT which is referable to the six month period before the order. This scenario may apply to a sole trader who has been made bankrupt.

● *Debts due in respect of social security contributions* Sums due from the debtor covering social security contributions deducted from staff pay in respect of various contributions under Class 1 or Class 2 payments for a period of 12 months before the order.

● *Debts due in respect of occupational pension schemes, etc.* Sums due from the employer to which Schedule 4 of the Pension Schemes Act 1993 applies (contributions to occupational and state scheme premiums).

● *Remuneration of employees* Any amount owed to an employee which:

(a) is owed by the debtor to a person who is or has been an employee of the debtor; and

(b) is payable by way of remuneration in respect of the whole or any part of the period of four months next before the relevant date. There is at present a limit of £800 per employee in this context.

Remuneration above includes accrued holiday remuneration. Furthermore, the schedule states that amounts falling under (a) and (b) above include 'so much of any sum owed in respect of money advanced for the purpose as has been applied for the payment of a debt which, if it had not been paid, would have been a debt falling within the above paragraph' (i.e. preferential). Thus, if a lender advances money to a debtor in order that the debtor can pay his wages bill to staff, such a loan in the books of the lender will be preferential. Two points emerge here.

Firstly, the statute (the Insolvency Act 1986) gives force to the doctrine of subrogation in favour of the lender. This well established principle has long been with us and indeed it has an interesting and helpful application in the field of corporate insolvency whereupon a lender, e.g. a bank, advances money to a corporate borrower for payment of the company wage bill. However, this topic will be enlarged upon in Chapter 16.

Secondly, the concept of wages forming part of the list of preferential debts in an individual insolvency is new. The provisions stated and explained above form part of the Insolvency Act 1986. Previously, preferential debt provisions were split between the Bankruptcy Act 1914 and the (then) current Companies Act 1948 in such a way that the wages concept applied only to corporate insolvency cases. Now both individual and corporate situations are dealt with under the umbrella of the Insolvency Act 1986 and the wages concept now applies equally well to the insolvency of the individual, the company or indeed the partnership.

It may be said that establishing a preferential claim by a creditor in an individual insolvency is more clear cut than would be the case in a corporate winding up. For a start, the juxtaposition of the preferential claim against the equitable interests of the floating chargee is a question of anguish to many creditors in a corporate winding up. This will be covered in depth later (see Chapter 15). However, a further query arises in a corporate winding up where a creditor has two debts owing by the debtor – one preferential and one ordinary – together with a credit balance showing a sum owed by the creditor to the bankrupt company. This is by no means an esoteric example. This matter is bound up with the rules covering the statutory availability of set-off of credit balances against an overdraft or loan in the hands of a banker to the debtor who is now bankrupt. All preferential creditors must be subject to the *pari passu* rule that equal treatment must be afforded to every preferential creditor by the trustee. Within this (or any other) class of creditors there are no subdivisions of interest.

Ordinary creditors

Ordinary creditors usually form the main bulk of creditors by number who are neither secured nor preferential (or, in the case of a company, the holders of a floating charge). These creditors are also treated equally and are the ones who, because of the very nature of the debtor's insolvency, can hardly expect a handsome return of their debts.

Deferred creditors

Provision is made in the Act s. 329 for yet another class of creditor – the deferred creditor. It is stated that a debt owed by the bankrupt to a person, whether or not that person was the bankrupt's spouse at the time the loan was made, is the spouse of the bankrupt at the time of the bankruptcy order. This creditor shall be paid last in priority after the ordinary creditors have been paid in full.

Before the generality of the bankrupt's estate can be finally assessed and what, if anything, each class of creditor may expect to receive in due course from the trustee can be calculated, certain other matters have to be taken into account.

Creditors' rights of set-off

Practical difficulties arise on the liquidation of a company in relation to creditors' rights of set-off, but the underlying principles apply as well to the estate of the individual bankrupt. Indeed, the basic rule is given in s. 323, which is the part of the Act covering individual bankruptcy as distinct from corporate insolvency. It is thus necessary to examine the rule here and, for the sake of completeness, to cover by way of example the corporate situation as well.

Section 323 is worth repeating in full:

> (1) This section applies where before the commencement of the bankruptcy there have been mutual credits, mutual debits or other mutual dealings between the bankrupt and any creditor of the bankrupt proving or claiming to prove for a bankruptcy debt.

> (2) An account shall be taken of what is due from each party to the other in respect of the mutual dealings and the sums due from one party shall be set off against the sums due from the other.

> (3) Sums due from the bankrupt to another party shall not be included in the account taken under subsection (2) if that other party had notice at the time they became due that a bankruptcy petition relating to the bankrupt was pending.

(4) Only the balance (if any) of the account taken under subsection (2) is provable as a bankruptcy debt or, as the case may be, to be paid to the trustee as part of the bankrupt's estate.

These rules are a carry-over from those given in the old Bankruptcy Act 1914 s. 31 although some subtle changes have taken place. Even so, it could be said that they are not completely clear. In addition, some aspects of set-off have since been clarified by case decision.

Example: Set-off of bank accounts of the debtor

As bankers are well aware the right of set-off, that is 'combination' of a customer's debit and credit balances, is well documented. Balances may be set off at any appropriate time provided such accounts are 'due' (which may exclude the term loan). Each account in the set-off exercise must be in the same right and name(s). An overdraft in the names of Mr and Mrs Smith could be set off against a credit balance in the name of either party on sole account by virtue of the 'joint and several' clause in the account mandate form taken by the banker when the account opened. However, a debit balance in the sole name of one party could not be set off against a credit balance in joint names. In addition, a debit balance in the sole name of Mr Smith could not be set off against an account styled 'Mr Smith – Tennis Club a/c' since the bank is on notice as a constructive trustee that the credit funds are not in reality the property of Mr Smith. These rules apply also to the insolvency situation.

Where the debtor is subject to a bankruptcy order, the rules of s. 323 of the Act apply in addition to the common law rules quoted above, which are outside the bankruptcy rules as such. The insolvency application of set-off is termed the 'statutory right of set-off'. It may be said that the statutory rules extend the common law rules. The creditor of a bankrupt debtor does not have to make a decision as to whether to set off or not. The application of s. 323 makes it a mandatory act. The question of what sums are due takes on important meaning. Outside bankruptcy, the creditor cannot set off credit balances against a contingent debt in his books.

By way of example (using a corporate example, although the sole trader in bankruptcy would face similar considerations), let us suppose that the books of Big Bank plc show the following position of J Bloggs Ltd when notice of petition is received:

No. 1 current account:	£30 000 credit
No. 2 current account:	£200 000 debit
Deposit account at 60 days' notice:	£90 000 credit
Loan account at 90 days' term:	£50 000 debit
Discount account:	£30 000 debit

Let us assume for the sake of simplicity that the deposit and loan accounts both have three weeks still to run.

The overall net position in the bank's books is £130 000 (actual) debit plus contingent liability of £30 000 which (if it materialises) brings the total net indebtedness to £160 000. The problem now is: what is the bank's position *vis-à-vis* the liquidator concerning the various liabilities of J Bloggs Ltd? The best scenario for the bank would be to set off everything as follows:

Total credit balances (£30 000 + £90 000)	= £120 000
Total debit balances (£200 000 + £50 000 + £30 000)	= £280 000
Net debit, which prove in the liquidation	= £160 000

The worst scenario for the bank would probably be where total credit balances which are claimed by the liquidator are £120 000 and J Bloggs Ltd is in debt to the bank for a total of £250 000. If the discount proves to be bad (the discounted bill is unpaid on maturity) a further £30 000 would be owing, bringing the bank's claim to a figure of £280 000.

The practical effects of the Insolvency Act

Section 323 produces some useful rules for the creditor. The two claims for set-off need not be of the same type. Thus, unlike the case with common law situations, unliquidated claims may be set off against a liquidated debt and perhaps a contingent debt. Some doubt has been expressed in the legal world concerning the exact status here of the contingent debt. For one example, the complicated decision in *Re Charge Card Services Ltd* (1986), such hope of set-off is real. The whole essence of set-off claim was examined in depth in the decision of *National Westminster Bank* v *Halesowen Pressworks & Assemblies Ltd* (1972) (which used s. 31 of the Bankruptcy Act 1914 as the base). In that decision it was stated 'it [set-off] arose to prevent the injustice of such a man having to pay in full what he owed in respect of such dealings [mutual dealings between him and the counterparty, who is now in bankruptcy] while only receiving a dividend on what the bankrupt owed him in respect of them'. In the J Bloggs Ltd example, suppose that there had been credit funds available to meet the cost of the discounted bill on non-payment (which there was not) and such funds had already been paid to the liquidator. The bank would have surrendered credit funds available and been left to prove as an unsecured creditor in respect of the value of the unpaid bill, which had been discounted 'with recourse to the debtor'. That might be considered unjust. It is thought safe to set off the contingent debt against credit funds, if available (or at least put the point forcibly to the liquidator).

One point, which is more certain, surrounds the fixed deposit and the fixed loan. In the normal way (excluding insolvency) such sums are not available under the rules of common law for set-off unless they are due, i.e. either the time has run out on the depositor or – more likely in the case of the loan – the borrower has defaulted under the terms of the loan contract. The loan will thus become due immediately. However, as was demonstrated forcibly by the *Halesowen* decision (referred to above) when insolvency proceedings commence, the original contract – the loan facility letter – is itself accelerated, i.e. the loan becomes due. One could argue that once a petition is grounded for a winding up the normal banker–customer relationship has ceased and instead there is a liquidator–banker relationship.

Under these rules, in the case of J Bloggs Ltd the bank would exercise its statutory right to set off and prove as an unsecured creditor for the amount of £130 000 (and if the bill turns out to be bad, a further £30 000).

A further complication can however arise where, for example, it transpires that mixed in with a debit balance on current account (e.g. J Bloggs Ltd No 2 account) there are wages cheques for recent company wage payments. The examination of the account utilising the rules in *Clayton's* case of 1816 may reveal such cheques. Bearing in mind that the rights of the creditor to set off in other circumstances than insolvency were examined in the case of *Re William Hall (Contractors) Ltd* (1967), the outcome is different where insolvency has reared its head. In those circumstances a creditor banker may well wish to set off any credit monies all to non-preferential debts and thus leave the maximum possible preferential claim intact. The liquidator will have a very different view. This difficulty has been settled very equitably in the decision *Re Unit 2 Windows Ltd* (1985). The rule now is that where a creditor has two claimable debts – one preferential and one non-preferential – and a credit balance for set-off, the credit monies must be set off against both debts rateably, i.e. in proportion to the debt figures before set-off takes place. If a banker has opened a wages account before the petition this whole matter takes on a larger perspective. However, this aspect will be covered in more depth later (see Chapter 16).

Non-provable debts

The Insolvency Rules 1986 number 12.3 specifies that all claims by creditors are provable against the bankrupt, whether they are present or future, certain or contingent, ascertained or sounding only in damages. However, certain debts form an exception to this rule and thus are not provable in bankruptcy, e.g.

- any fine imposed for an offence and any obligation arising under an order made in family or domestic proceedings;
- any obligation arising under a confiscation order made under s. 1 of the Drug Trafficking Offences Act 1986.

Fines and maintenance payments must always be paid in full by the bankrupt and thus there is no need for them to be proved in bankruptcy.

Certain debts, e.g. illegal debts, foreign tax claims and statute barred debts are not available for proof.

Interest on debts

A creditor who is proving in the bankruptcy for repayment of his debt may include interest at the contracted rate up until the time of the bankruptcy order (Insolvency Rules number 6.113). Under s. 328 of the Act once an order is made interest may only accrue on the debt thereafter at the higher rate of either that specified in the underlying contract or the statutory rate. Nevertheless, interest applicable to the debt from the date of the bankruptcy order may only be paid once all preferential and ordinary debts have been repaid from the estate in full (this includes payment of interest on preferential debts after the order date).

The distribution of the estate by the trustee

The trustee has to write to all known creditors requesting claims where the creditors have not yet submitted claim forms. The notice will specify the last date for proving debts. This must be at least 21 days ahead of the date of the notice. Unless creditors have been invited to prove debts by public advertisement, notice of intended dividend will be given in this way. The trustee can give a date by which all claims must be submitted and he can stick to that date, although he is free to admit late claims if he so desires. The notice of dividend will show details of all realisations, fees paid, etc. and the total amount to be distributed (Insolvency Rules number 11).

The Act s. 324 refers to the manner in which the bankrupt's estate shall be distributed. The trustee is obliged to retain sufficient monies in his care to cater for:

- any debts which seem to be due to persons who reside so far away that they have not had sufficient time to establish their proofs;
- any monies which may be needed to settle claims which have still to be determined;
- any disputed claims or proofs.

In addition the trustee must retain sufficient monies to cover the expenses of the bankruptcy, including his fees.

Section 328 (3) specifies the order of payout:

(1) The expenses and fees of the trustee. This sum can come as quite a shock to the unsecured creditor. With regard to the trustee's fees, the rules can be found in the Insolvency Rules numbers 4.127 and 6.138. The calculation may be based on either the percentage of realisations or simply on time costs. The trustee's fees will generally be agreed by the creditors' committee or, if there is not one, the creditors themselves at the first creditors' meeting.

(2) The preferential debts (see page 85).

(3) The ordinary creditors (see page 87).

(4) The deferred creditors, if any (see page 88).

Finally, under the terms of the Act s. 331, the trustee shall summon a final meeting of creditors at which he will produce his report containing details of the winding up and the outcome of his endeavours.

PART THREE

The insolvent partnership

CHAPTER NINE
The bankrupt firm

The rules

Rules covering the winding up of the insolvent partnership are now contained in the Insolvent Partnerships Order 1994 (SI 1994/2421). This statutory instrument, which came into force on 1 December 1994, revokes and replaces the Insolvent Partnerships Order 1986 (SI 1986/2142). This somewhat complex area of insolvency law is simplified by the fact that the schedules to the order set out the modified provisions in full. The Insolvent Partnerships Order 1994 (IPO 94 Part I) applies as follows:

(a) in the case of insolvency proceedings in relation to companies and partnerships, relates to companies and partnerships which courts in England and Wales have jurisdiction to wind up; and

(b) in the case of insolvency proceedings in relation to individuals, extends to England and Wales only.

Thus the court may now hear a creditor's petition against a partnership if the debt on which the petition is based arises where the respective firm's place of business which generated the contract is in the jurisdiction. This is so even if the partnership's principal place of business is located outside the jurisdiction.

The emphasis is now on the business's whereabouts rather than the situation of its assets.

The modified provisions referred to above are taken from the Insolvency Act 1986 as appropriate and drafted to suit the insolvent partnership situation.

Legal status of the partnership

Before the various aspects of the insolvency of the partnership or its partners are considered it may be helpful to mention the specific legal status enjoyed by the partnership under English law. The Partnership Act 1890 s. 1 defines the partnership as follows:

Partnership is the relationship which subsists between persons carrying on a business in common with a view of profit.

The above definition is surely loaded. Every word is vital. The partnership is a relationship. This indicates that it is not a separate entity in its own right (unlike the situation under United States or Scottish law). The relationship is 'business' in its make up. Partners work together with a view to profit even though on occasion a trading loss is achieved. It thus follows that a partnership firm in England and Wales does not have a distinct corporate personality of its own. There is no veil of incorporation, such as shrouds the incorporated limited company. This basic legal principle became clear with the decision in *Salomon* v *Salomon & Co Ltd* (1897). It is true that the legal status of the company as a distinct body is subject to necessary caveats as enunciated in the case of *Foss* v *Harbottle* (1843) some 54 years before the *Salomon* case brought matters to a head. The shareholder/director of a company cannot exactly hide behind the corporate veil to further his personal position at the expense of minority members or to cloak more sinister activities. Even so, this basic difference between the partnership and the incorporated company prevails to this day.

Legal status of the partner

The legal status of a partner, that is his rights and duties *vis-à-vis* his fellow partners and the outside world, is laid down in the partnership deed if there is one. If there is no deed – or if the deed is silent on a point – then the provisions of the Partnership Act 1890 are brought to bear. For example:

● All partners are entitled to share equally in profits and contribute equally towards losses (s. 24 (1)).

● The partnership will be dissolved (not bankrupted) upon the bankruptcy of any one partner, unless otherwise agreed (s. 33 (1)).

● Every partner in a firm is liable jointly with the other partners (s. 9).

Superimposed on the provisions of the Partnership Act 1890 is the IPO 94. It may be that the fact that this intricate area of the law is best suited to legislation by decree is a benefit to the commercial community in that a measure of speed and flexibility is present.

The procedures for winding up

The procedures for winding up a firm or bankrupting one or more partners – as laid out in the IPO 94 – draw on the provisions of the Insolvency Act 1986 (as modified and laid out in the order). Insolvent partnerships have been treated as unregistered companies for winding up purposes since 1986. Thus, courts have been enabled to wind up insolvent firms as compulsory liquidations. The individual partners themselves are not necessarily involved in insolvency proceedings against their personal estates. Depending on whether the partners are corporate or individual partners there is a range of possible permutations in the IPO 94.

The IPO 94 specifies the following combinations of rules.

Creditors' winding up petitions

Winding up of insolvent partnership as unregistered company on petition of creditor, etc. where no concurrent petition is presented against a member

or

winding up of insolvent partnership as unregistered company on creditor's petition where concurrent petitions are presented against one or more members.

Members' petitions

Winding up of insolvent partnership as unregistered company on member's petition where no concurrent petition is presented against a

member
>   or

winding up of insolvent partnership as unregistered company on member's petition where concurrent petitions are presented against all members
>   and

insolvency proceedings not involving winding up of insolvent partnership as unregistered company where individual members present joint bankruptcy petition.

The alternatives specified above take account of the diverse financial crises which may befall the firm and/or its members. The schedules to the IPO 94 as already stated set out the many procedural details of each option by translating specified sections of the Insolvency Act 1986 into minutiae applicable to the partnership scene.

Key points

Treatment of the joint estate of the firm and the separate estates of the members

Treatment of the joint estate of the firm and the separate estates of the members are seen to be salient points of the winding up of the partnership and insolvency of one or more members and the recommendations of the Cork Committee have finally been implemented in this respect. For many years the rule has been that each partner's estate must be settled *vis-à-vis* his private creditors in full before any private assets could be used in paying partnership debts. Under the current rules, where the joint estate is not sufficient to cover the joint debts the trustee or liquidator aggregates the balance of unsatisfied claims and can prove for that amount against the partners' separate estates. Such claims rank equally with other unsecured creditors. The preferential claims of creditors in the joint estate are not treated preferentially in the separate estates. However, if a dividend is received in the joint estate from a separate estate the usual rules as to preferential distribution apply to creditors of the joint estate. This new rule can make a dramatic difference to the chances of creditors in a complicated winding up of a firm with concurrent bankruptcy of one or more partners. For example, suppose a partnership of ABC and Co displays the following figures on becoming bankrupt:

assets: £200 000   liabilities: £450 000

and the private estate of A is currently:

assets: £200 000   liabilities: £100 000

Until 1994 the private creditors of A would have been paid in full.

Since the IPO 94, the partnership deficit of £250 000 will become a claim on A's private estate and thus A's creditors will receive just over half their debts. (This does not take account of the rights of contribution and subrogation of A towards B and C assuming that such claims in A's hands have a monetary value.)

This change in partnership winding up rules may well be of help to a firm's creditors who previously may have considered that enforcement of their debts against one or more of the partners' private estates would not be worth while in terms of cost of the action against likely returns.

Administration orders

Under the terms of the IPO 94 it is now possible for creditors of a partnership to initiate an administration order against the firm. Such an order operates substantially in the same manner as an administration order against a company.

Administration orders, which first became available to company creditors within the terms of the Insolvency Act 1986 and which now extend to partnerships, will allow an IP (the administrator) to continue the firm's business with a view to its survival or better realisation. Once an administration order is made, the firm is afforded significant protection against its creditors. Prior to 1994, a partnership which had become insolvent could only avoid liquidation by offering a voluntary arrangement for one or more partners individually, which then in turn dealt with partnership assets. This was often totally unsatisfactory for solving the problem and was in any case far too cumbersome for all but very small firms.

One major difference between the company administration order and that applicable to a partnership concerns the ability of the holder of a floating charge (e.g. the company's bankers) to veto the administration order through the medium of the administrative receiver appointed under the bank's floating charge. If the bank finds that in its opinion an administration order will not benefit the company's position (never mind that of the bank) such action by the bank (i.e. the veto) is surely justified. Even if the bank does permit the administration order, the question may arise as to who will pay the costs of the administration if there is not a flow of income available to the company. The IPO 94 recognises that the giving of floating charges is foreign to partnerships. Thus banks will not be able to block the appointment of an administration order over a firm.

One exception to the above is recognised in the IPO 94 and that relates to those circumstances where a partnership has taken agricultural credits. A secured creditor of a firm may have power to appoint an administrative receiver under the terms of the Agricultural Credits Act 1928 and thus block the appointment of an administration order. Whilst the holder of an agricultural charge can combine fixed and floating security, the analogy with a company debenture is hardly complete. The agricultural charge can only be taken over specified classes of asset which may form only part of the firm's estate. The IPO 94 does not require the receivership appointment to relate to the whole, or substantially the whole, of the firm's assets. It may be said that such lightweight charges will become more common over firms' assets. Even so this is only a problem for the agricultural sector.

The company voluntary arrangement

The IPO 94 introduced the possibility of the partnership entering into a company voluntary arrangement (CVA). This procedure has been available to the insolvent individual and the insolvent company since 1986 but hitherto not to the partnership. Now the firm may put its proposals to a meeting of creditors and, if approval is obtained from over 75% in value of the creditors present and voting in person or by proxy, such arrangement may be put into effect. Corporate arrangements are covered elsewhere (see page 110). The CVA, once approved, will bind all creditors who were given notice of and entitled to vote at the meeting.

It is hoped that the CVA route will prove beneficial for the partnership. One problem is that for the CVA to work effectively it must bind all creditors. To date, difficulties have arisen with CVAs concerning limited companies and such problems will now impinge onto partnership firms entering this route. Under the Act a creditor may not vote in respect of an unliquidated claim except where the chairman (the nominee) agrees to put upon the debt an estimated minimum value for the purposes of entitlement to vote. The recent case *Re Cranley Mansions Ltd* (1994) showed that agreement must be present amongst creditors which requires 'some element of bilateral concurrence between the chairman of the meeting and the creditor in question'. If a creditor has no entitlement to vote at the meeting it seems to follow that the creditor shall not be bound by the terms of any CVA and he appears to have a choice as to whether, as a creditor with an unliquidated or unascertained debt, he does or does not wish to be bound by the CVA. A fair conclusion seems to be that the concept of the chairman's willingness to put an estimated minimum value on the debt (thus allowing the creditor to vote) contrasts somewhat with the requirement for some concurrence between the chairman and the creditor in question. This may all appear to be somewhat esoteric as a serious query but this set of circumstances may well cause significant problems at a creditors' meeting with regard to say the debtor's liability for future payments of rent. In order that the CVA may work efficiently, such problems – which may give rise to policy decisions – will, it is hoped, be clarified by future subordinate legislation.

Another significant problem concerning the future working of the partnership CVA is that the procedure for firms follows that adopted under the Act for corporate and not individual insolvent debtors. The partnership CVA has no provision for an interim order to be obtained. Some say that this provision would benefit the corporate and the partnership situation. Without this important facility the firm may be too vulnerable to its creditors during the period when the CVA proposals are being considered. At present, a solution may be that a partner of an insolvent partnership may consider an IVA alongside the CVA so that some measure of protection at least can be afforded to the partnership's assets in the critical period before the CVA is approved by the firm's creditors. The IPO 94 does not allow the partners' private estates to be included in any arrangement sought by the firm. However, it is perfectly possible for the partners to use the IVA procedure alongside the firm's CVA in order that all estates may be covered at the same time.

The partner's position

The IPO 94 s. 16 states that where an insolvent partnership is wound up as an unregistered company, the partners concerned are subject to the provisions of the Company Directors Disqualification Act 1986 and are thus subject to the rules covering delinquent directors of companies – charges of fraudulent and wrongful trading come to mind as well as the disabilities of directors caught by the rules. It will now be possible for a partner of a liquidated firm to be banned from holding office as a director or manager of any company for a given period. It does not seem clear from the IPO 94 that such a partner will be banned from becoming a partner in another partnership.

The future of the Insolvent Partnerships Order

The IPO 94 should be given a cautious welcome. The various problems which have been mentioned above will hopefully disappear over time. Perhaps a further IPO will emerge to address various problems attendant on the new procedures. The lack of a moratorium in a firm's CVA may be seen as a particularly pressing problem. The responses from various professional bodies to member firms following the CVA or administration order routes may be of critical importance to the development of current partnership insolvency practice. The extension of the corporate culture to partnerships could be beneficial, provided that the special attributes of the partnership are respected.

PART FOUR

Corporate insolvency

CHAPTER TEN

Introduction to corporate insolvency

The law regarding the insolvency of a limited company in England and Wales has developed along with the growth of the company as such. Whilst the large joint stock company – never mind the multinational conglomerate – is essentially a twentieth century phenomenon, the origins of this matter lie in the history of the growth of commerce in the United Kingdom. For many years the law covering the winding up of a company was to be found (to a large extent) in the current substantive Companies Act (amended perhaps by a subsequent amending Act). However, corporate insolvency is now covered in the Act along with the rules of individual insolvency. Other important and relevant pieces of legislation such as the Company Directors Disqualification Act 1986 run alongside the Act.

Limited liability of the company

The first Joint Stock Companies Act was passed in 1844. Until that time the shareholders of the 'company' had unlimited liability for the company's debts and there was little difference in practice between the insolvent liquidation of the company and the bankruptcy of the individual. Once the concept of limited liability of shareholders was introduced in 1844 the whole manner of the winding up of a company had to be restated. The principle of the 'veil of incorporation' already referred to (see page 20), which was further developed with the case of *Salomon* v *Salomon & Co Ltd* (1897) provided vital new thinking. Thus there developed two main ways of winding up a company which cater for both the situation of the company and that of the shareholders. These are:

- the voluntary liquidation;
- the compulsory liquidation.

Types of corporate liquidation

A company may wish to wind up as a solvent entity. This procedure is known as the 'members' voluntary winding up'. The main legal rule here is that the directors must file declarations of solvency whereby the authorities ensure as far as possible that the company taking this route is in fact solvent so that all creditors will receive their money back in full. The mechanics of this form of winding up are outside the basic rules of insolvency. An insolvent company may still be wound up without the direct involvement of the court by means of the 'creditors' voluntary winding up' process. Here, the creditors, who after all are the persons most concerned in the winding up, have control over the whole matter. There was at one time also a halfway house called a 'members' voluntary liquidation subject to the supervision of the court' which is no longer possible. Indeed, such a course has been left out of the Act. The compulsory liquidation, which is based on a court order, is the alternative to the creditors' voluntary liquidation. Both types of liquidation will be considered in detail later (see Chapter 14).

Alternatives to full liquidation

Current insolvency legislation allows for alternative routes towards full liquidation in much the same manner as is provided for the individual. The Cork Committee suggested that much of the detail of insolvency procedure for companies and individual debtors be brought together and thus some distinctions between the two have now disappeared. This has made the procedures much simpler for the insolvency industry to manage. More important is the fact that the company which is technically insolvent (or about to become so) has specified alternative routes. Creditors of companies have a choice of legal and practical positions to adopt towards insolvent companies. It is now appropriate to examine this area in some depth before consideration is given to the winding up of the insolvent company.

The main legal courses for a creditor or an insolvent company to follow are:

● the company voluntary arrangement;

● the administration order;

● the appointment of a receiver under the Law of Property Act 1925 or the appointment of an administrative receiver under the Insolvency Act 1986 (see Chapter 12).

These options are considered in detail in Chapters 11–13.

Clearly the above alternatives can only apply in given circumstances and depend to some extent on the wishes and abilities of both the creditors and the company (to say nothing of the attitude, in certain cases, of the court). The point is that once again the 'Cork philosophy' shines through and the system has the overriding aim of supporting a recovery scenario where such is apposite. It should be borne in mind that the scene is fast moving and is changing rapidly. It might have been thought that the fundamental legislation and reform provided by the package of legislation in 1986 would allow the business community to adopt the view that consolidation and stability would now reign. This does not appear to be so and the DTI consultative document 'Company voluntary arrangements and administration orders' issued 9 November 1993 promises once again to bring fundamental change to the scene. Certainly there is cause for concern in the document in respect of certain classes of creditors, e.g. the lending banker who is secured by a floating charge over the assets of the corporate borrower. This is as yet only a consultative document and the end product is a matter of speculation. A further consultative document covering certain corporate matters is currently under consideration.

CHAPTER ELEVEN

The company voluntary arrangement

Definition

The company voluntary arrangement (CVA) is in many ways akin to the individual voluntary arrangement (IVA) and is, broadly speaking, geared to the same objectives. The rules covering the CVA are to be found in the Act ss. 1–7 inclusive as further explained by the Rules numbers 1.1–1.30 inclusive.

The CVA is basically an agreement between a company and the shareholders and directors of that company for a scheme or composition (or both in part) whereby the repayment of the debts of the company is delayed or settled at less than 100 pence in the pound. This is done on a structured basis under the control of an IP. It may well transpire that the company (or part of it) survives its current financial troubles, although ultimate liquidation may well ensue. In that event it is hoped that the creditors would still come away with more of their debts repaid than may have been the case had liquidation been instituted at the outset.

The CVA proposal

Initially the CVA may be proposed either by the directors of a company (provided that the company is not already in administration or winding up procedure) or, where insolvency proceedings are in being, by the administrator or liquidator (the Act s. 1). The CVA may thus provide the turning point for the company's fortunes in that it proves to be a halfway house between financial trauma (the administration or winding up) and ultimate recovery. The involvement of the court in a CVA process is seen as minimal. The Act and the Rules provide detailed rules of procedure and specify rights of creditors, etc.

Procedure

Where other insolvency procedures are not in train, the directors of the company must prepare detailed proposals for the CVA. At this point the company would already be in serious trouble in that it is either insolvent or likely to become so in the near future. No doubt the directors would be seriously concerned with the position and aware of not only the rights of the creditors but also their own liabilities and the possibility that they might later be charged with wrongful or fraudulent trading. In other words the directors will consider in depth any possible way ahead for the company. The advice of the company's solicitors, accountants and bankers will very likely be obtained and there will be some serious board meetings. It may well be that the CVA is wholly inappropriate as a recovery vehicle for a particular company in a given situation, as will be discussed later (see page 118). If the CVA is indeed seen as being appropriate the set routine action is decided upon. If the company is already under the control of an administrator or is in course of winding up and thus is being controlled by an IP, different considerations apply. Then the administrator or liquidator must consider that the company is – under their guidance and no doubt with the goodwill of the creditors – being turned around to the point where a revival is called for free from the rigours of court orders. Ultimately the company (or the profitable part of it) may be brought back to normality.

The directors and liquidator or administrator (as appropriate) will draw up a set of proposals which must eventually be lodged at court. Where the proposals are being drawn up by the directors they must approach an IP and obtain his approval of the arrangement and agreement to act as nominee of the CVA. The nominee, who is proposed by the board, signifies agreement to act by endorsing a copy of the notice to act. This is then dated and returned to the directors.

Contents of the proposal

The proposal must contain details of the company's position and is crucial to the success of the whole operation. The Rules number 1.3 lists all the points which have to be covered in the proposal, the most important being:

● Why is a CVA desired and why would it benefit the creditors such that they would agree to it?

● Details must be provided of all company assets and whether any such assets are already charged to creditors or are to be excluded from the CVA.

● How are the liabilities of the company, which must be shown in detail, to be met and paid? In addition, how are the preferential creditors to be dealt with? How are creditors who are connected with the company to be treated?

● Are the directors aware of any transactions of the company which, if the company was to go into liquidation, would be treated as transactions at undervalue, preferences, extortionate credit transactions, or even invalid floating charges? If such circumstances have been identified by the directors then a clear statement of intention is needed as to what provision will be made in the CVA for wholly or partly indemnifying the company in respect of such claims.

● What, if any, guarantees have been given by third parties over the company's debts and are such guarantors connected persons of the company?

● Dates and proposed distributions to creditors are required as well as the estimated timescale of the CVA.

● Details are to be given of the amounts envisaged to be paid to the nominee and the supervisor by way of expenses and fees.

● It must be stated whether any directors are expected to offer guarantees behind the arrangement and if so what security, if any, is being offered to cover such guarantees.

● The manner in which funds are to be held during the CVA operation must be declared and how the business is to be conducted during the period of the CVA.

● Details of any credit facilities to be raised during the CVA and methods of repayment of such monies are to be given.

● The specific functions of the supervisor during the period of the CVA must be described and details of such persons provided.

Note that the proposal may be amended at any time until delivery to court provided that any amendment is made in writing by the nominee. The above list may appear at first to be all embracing. The information required under the Rules should enable the creditors to arrive at a decision as to the viability of the arrangement. It could be said that the information required in the proposal should be even more comprehensive, e.g. why are details not required of immediate cash flow in the form of a detailed statement or even details concerning the company's trading policy and the plans for the future when the CVA has run its course? Such additional information could, it may be argued, do even more to convince the creditors as to the course of action to take. However, creditors could presumably raise these points fully at meetings before they are expected to vote on the matter.

The practical meaning of the points required in the proposal is indeed revealing and the position of secured creditors is interesting. Unsecured creditors will not be impressed by the fact that the cream of the company's assets is already charged to a secured creditor, e.g. a mortgage on the main building might already be in place in favour of the company's bankers. In addition, the legal status of the unsecured creditors must be protected from the diminution of the company's asset base caused by transactions at undervalue, etc. as listed above. Any such declarations would presumably raise doubts as to whether the CVA would take off since creditors would want very specific assurances that any monies which have been unfairly disbursed by the company will be recovered by the supervisor for the benefit of the general body of unsecured creditors. Certainly the creditors will not agree to preferences, undervalues, etc. being forgotten when such transactions could be vigorously attacked by a liquidator in a winding up situation. Whether or not the liquidator would do this may well depend on the amount of money or assets the company has available to fight the case and the amount likely to be recovered. Once the nominee has received the directors' proposal he must within seven days obtain from them the full statement of affairs. The nominee shall have access to the company records if desired and the statement itself must be up to date, that is to within two weeks of the date he, the nominee, received notice to act.

Approach to court

Within 28 days from the date when the nominee returns the notice to the directors signifying his willingness to act, he must prepare and deliver to court his report. This will state whether he considers that meetings of the company and creditors should be convened and, if so, when and where. The proposal and report together with the statement are delivered to court and any director member or creditor may inspect the documentation.

Meetings

The Rules require the nominee to call meetings of shareholders and creditors (he may under rule number 1.21 combine the two meetings if he thinks fit). Meetings must be summoned within a timescale of 14 and 21 days from the date of filing the report at court. Likewise, 14 days' notice of a meeting must be given to all creditors. Documents mentioned above, e.g. the directors' proposal, the statement of affairs and the nominee's comments are forwarded with the meeting agenda. In addition, proxy forms are sent to all creditors. Where both creditors' and shareholders' meetings are convened, they are usually held on the same day with the creditors' meeting held first. In practical terms this is sensible as the shareholders' meeting would be to little effect if the creditors turned the scheme down or required radical changes to be made to proposals.

The conduct of both the creditors' and shareholders' meetings are covered in the Rules numbers 1.13 *et seq.* The creditors' meeting is conducted according to the following:

● The chairman is the convener, i.e. the nominee.

● The purpose of the meeting is to enable creditors to approve the voluntary arrangement as it stands, reject it or approve it with modifications.

● Voting procedure (this may seem somewhat involved in its application): firstly, secured creditors may only vote in respect of the unsecured portion of their debt, if any, remaining after the value of their security has been deducted from the total debt figure. This should not give rise to any difficulty. However, the rules then give what is in effect a dual voting rule. To pass a proposal (or a modification of it) a majority in excess of 75% in value of creditors present and voting in person or by proxy is required. (The rule does not attach the number of creditors voting as such.) The Rules number 1.19(2) then states:

> The same applies in respect of any other resolution proposed at the meeting, but substituting one half for three quarters.

It may not be clear what 'any other resolution' may be since presumably any modification of the proposal by definition must require the three-quarters majority. Perhaps an adjournment resolution would fall under this head.

Modifications to the proposal

The question of modifications may be a source of concern to creditors who initially approve an arrangement only to find later the scheme has been changed to their detriment. It may be that creditors are content with the original proposal and find they cannot attend the meeting. Later they may be somewhat surprised to learn the scheme is different to what they expected it to be. The Act ss. 4(1) and 4(2) throw some light on this problem:

> The meetings summoned under section 3 shall decide whether to approve the proposed voluntary arrangement (with or without modifications).

And:

> The modifications may include one conferring the functions proposed to be conferred on the nominee on another person qualified to act as an insolvency practitioner in relation to the company.

This section of the Act appears to suggest that one modification could be to change the nominee. It is clear that it must not change the arrangement to one that ceases to be a proposal such as is mentioned in s.1. All this is slightly vague and in these circumstances an aggrieved creditor has to rely on his rights of objection, which are covered below. Perhaps in the interests of fairness the Act avoids specific definition but this leaves the matter open to misinterpretation.

At the shareholders' meeting, voting rules are as defined in the Articles of the company. A simple majority is all that is usually necessary to carry a resolution.

Objections to the proposal

The Act s. 6 states the rules whereby objections may be lodged to any resolutions passed at the creditors' or shareholders' meeting(s). Valid objections may be made if it is considered that the voluntary arrangement unfairly prejudices the interests of a creditor or else some material irregularity has taken place with regard to either of the meetings. Such objections may be raise by any party who is entitled to vote at one of the meetings or by the nominee, administrator or liquidator (where applicable). Objections must be made to the court within 28 days of the chairman's report of the meetings being lodged at the court whereupon the court may, as stated in the Act s. 6 (4):

- revoke or suspend approvals given by meetings;
- direct the summoning of further meetings to consider a revised proposal.

Once the voluntary arrangement is approved by both the creditors and the shareholders the nominee becomes the supervisor. He sends a copy of the chairman's report on the meetings to the Registrar of Companies for filing. Thus, the CVA now becomes binding on all creditors who had notice of the meeting and were entitled to vote (whether or not they actually attended a meeting). The CVA is now in force and in as much as it is registered at the companies registry, knowledge of the CVA is available to anyone who cares to search the file. No further court hearing or approval is necessary.

The approved CVA

There is one possible loose end associated with the procedure. The strength of the CVA is that once it is approved (and any dissension procedure has been concluded) it is binding on all creditors. However, it cannot be binding on any creditors who were unknown before the meetings. The Act s. 5 (2)(b) states that the CVA 'binds every person who was entitled to vote at that meeting [creditors' meeting] as if he were a party to the voluntary arrangement'. What happens if further creditors appear after the CVA becomes binding? There could be complaints from contingent creditors or creditors whose debt was uncertain in amount and thus could not vote at the meeting. Perhaps it is not helpful to give too much thought to creditors who were not entitled to vote anyway, or those who were left out of account. Certainly one may conclude that the process of convening the creditors' meeting is crucial to the success of the whole operation. Provided that is correct, no doubt the supervisor can assuage any subsequent creditor who may appear on the scene and, if necessary, apply to court for directions under s. 7 of the Act.

The supervisor

Once the supervisor is installed he must keep proper accounts if he is to carry on business or realise assets, etc. At least once every 12 months he must prepare receipt and expenditure accounts and send copies to the court, companies registry, the company, creditors, auditors and all members bound by the CVA.

Once the CVA has run its course the supervisor must account to all creditors and members with full details of all activities to date and send copies to the Registrar of Companies and the court.

Where the company was initially in administration or liquidation and the CVA was initiated by the administrator or liquidator, the Act s. 5 (3) will apply. This states:

If the company is being wound up or an administration order is in force, the court may do one or both of the following, namely:

(a) by order stay all proceedings in the winding up or discharge the administration order;

(b) give such directions with respect to the conduct of the winding up or the administration as it thinks appropriate for facilitating the implementation of the approved voluntary arrangement.

Thus, whereas one can say that the involvement of the court in the CVA initiated by the creditors is minimal (indeed it is in reality simply a place where copies of the documentation are available for inspection) court involvement where the company is already in insolvency at the outset is somewhat more evident. The winding up or administration of the company is not rescinded but simply stayed.

In addition, s. 7 (4) of the Act shows that:

The supervisor:

(a) may apply to court for directions in relation to any particular matter arising under the voluntary arrangement and

(b) is included among the persons who may apply to the court for the winding up of the company or for an administration order to be made in relation to it.

There is thus ample provision for the supervisor to exercise his functions to the full in the knowledge that if the CVA fails he has the necessary power to pass the company's affairs to the court for appropriate treatment.

Practical considerations

It is necessary to recognise an important difference between the IVA and the CVA. This is simply that with the CVA there is no court interim order once the proposal is lodged at court. Even so, this matter is under consideration by the DTI. The company's creditors will not be paralysed until a later stage in the proceedings. The Act does not provide that actions of creditors against a company must be stayed pending meetings of the shareholders and creditors. This may inhibit the directors of a company from seeking a CVA as they probably would not wish to cause the creditors to panic at the knowledge that a CVA is being sought and use the interim period to initiate liquidation proceedings. The directors may therefore institute an administration order (see Chapter 13) at the outset, in order for the company to obtain the protection it offers until the CVA is put to shareholders and members.

Use of the CVA

It may be interesting and helpful at this point to consider how useful a CVA may be. The CVA is relatively straightforward to institute and operate. In the United Kingdom the CVA presupposes that a company which is insolvent, or nearly so, is nevertheless capable of being revived and that it goes without saying that the directors are honest and desirous of affording the creditors the best and fairest treatment possible within any situation. The CVA, which was initiated by the Insolvency Act 1986, follows in many respects the path of Chapter 11 of the United States Bankruptcy Code.

It is suggested that in England suitable cases for a CVA would encompass the following scenarios:

- The position of the company should not be hopeless. Debts will most likely be paid in the long run. The hopeless concern is not suitable for CVA treatment.

● The company's troubles should have commenced recently and, for example, be the result of, say, the loss of one or two major clients. Such circumstances could possibly be rectified without full liquidation.

● The management should be competent and not need extensive supervision. The company should not have gone wrong through the directors' faulty or careless management techniques. There should be no hint of wrongful trading.

● Ideally the company should not be too large. The application of a CVA to a large multinational corporation could be difficult to say the least.

● It is preferable if the creditors are co-operative. Any agreement struck with them must be allowed to go through unhindered if the CVA is to work.

The future of the CVA route is interesting as the current DTI initiative – if approved and enacted – could well lead to a much greater use of the CVA than at present. Time will tell whether there is any evidence of the enhanced popularity of the CVA.

CHAPTER TWELVE

Receivership

Circumstances often impel the secured creditors of an ailing company to seek the appointment of a receiver, who will protect and possibly realise the creditors' security.

There are currently three main types of receiver:

(1) The receiver appointed under the terms of the Law of Property Act 1925 s. 101 (the LPA receiver).

(2) The receiver appointed by the court under the Companies Act 1985.

(3) The receiver appointed by a creditor who is secured by a debenture which contains a floating charge, i.e. the 'administrative' receiver.

In the context of this work it is necessary to cover the aspects relating to point (3) in full. Indeed it may be asked whether the appointment of an LPA receiver is really an insolvency matter as such. That type of receiver may well be appointed quite apart from situations where the debtor is insolvent although insolvency may intervene in due course. It is therefore apposite to cover point (1) in overview. The court-appointed receiver under the Companies Act 1985 (the 'Pendente Lite') is rare and it is not considered fruitful to pursue that matter here.

The receiver appointed under the provisions of the Law of Property Act 1925

A lender who has the security of a mortgage over property of the borrower has the statutory power under the LPA 1925 s. 101 to pursue one (or more) of the following remedies. He may:

- sue for repayment;
- foreclose (court order);
- sell;
- appoint a receiver;
- enter possession.

The application of the remedies listed differ, according to the type of mortgage, i.e. whether the mortgage is taken in legal or equitable form. In addition, the remedy of sale is subject to several case decisions as to timing and effect and that of 'taking possession' is also bound by statute which protects tenants against unfair eviction, etc. The efficacy of a mortgage is governed to a considerable extent by its type *vis-à-vis* current legal rules as well as by wording of the clauses of the document.

Creditors' rights

The right of the creditor who is secured by a mortgage over the property of a debtor to appoint a receiver under the LPA 1925 is dependent upon the statutory power in the Act, which may be varied or extended in the mortgage deed. The mortgage form employed by a lending bank may specify that rights of sale apply once the bank has made formal demand for repayment of the debt and any time allowed has run out. The bank's form will usually exclude the provisions of ss. 93 and 103 of the LPA 1925, thus permitting the bank to consolidate two or more mortgages it holds from the same customer and removing waiting periods for sale following the customer's default on the loan.

The so called Property Act receiver may have extensive powers enumerated in the mortgage deed, e.g. he may have powers to take possession, sell the property, lease it and so forth. His duties are also considerable, e.g. he collects rents, he ensures the insurances and repairs on the property are up to date and in order and he discharges rents, taxes and outgoings affecting the property.

The charging document, e.g. the form of mortgage, may in addition give the receiver powers to manage the property on a commercial basis over and above those powers laid down in statute.

The LPA receiver need not be an IP and thus may well be a chartered surveyor who will, as receiver, be concerned to collect rents from the property charged.

This remedy, i.e. the appointment of an LPA receiver, may often be taken by a secured lender, e.g. a bank which has unsuccessfully made formal demand for repayment of the debt secured by the property in question and which does not wish to sell the building for the time being or does not wish to pursue any of the other remedies available to the mortgagee. Thus, it may well be advisable for the secured bank to appoint a receiver over, say, a block of flats or offices which may be wholly or in part occupied by tenants. The sale of such property may be commercially ill advised as the receiver may see the income generated from the rents as being adequate (after outgoings) to fund a gradual repayment of the bank's debt.

The administrative receiver

The administrative receiver (AR) must be a licensed IP. The Act ss. 28–49 cover the rules concerning the AR in England and Wales. Section 29 (2) of the Act contains a definition of the AR as follows:

> A receiver or manager of the whole (or substantially the whole) of a company's property appointed by or on behalf of the holders of any debentures secured by a charge which, as created, was a floating charge, or by such a charge and one or more other securities.

The bank debenture

It will be apparent that the majority of administrative receiverships are initiated by banks holding floating charges over the debtor customer's property. The bank's debenture is in itself a complicated document to say the least and in its simpler form encapsulates a fixed charge over the company's fixed assets and a floating charge over the remainder of the undertaking, i.e. any subsequently acquired fixed assets or the current assets. This document, the so called Buckley agreement, is tailored to the asset side of the borrowing company's balance sheet and may well grant the bank fixed charges over some of the company's current assets, e.g. book debts. There is a wealth of case law applicable to such documents and deeper consideration of the finer points of the bank's debenture is outside the scope of this work. The appointment of an AR by the trustees under the issue of secured debentures in series is of course current, although not so common in practice as the appointment under the bank's Buckley agreement.

In short, the situation arises whereby a lending bank which has a form of debenture covering in various ways the assets of the borrowing company may well not wish to sell the company assets at a loss and indeed may see the continued running of the company (under the managership of an independent and qualified IP) as the proper option to take. The eventual sale of the business, or parts of it, may then become a viable option. It may be said that, whilst the AR procedure is in theory a rescue operation, it frequently falls short of that objective.

The appointment of the administrative receiver

The Act s. 33 guides the appointment of the AR. The appointment must be accepted by the appointee by the end of the day after that on which the letter of appointment is received by him. Failure to effect valid appointment may cause the appointer (the bank) to have to indemnify the appointee for damages caused by the invalid letter or procedure. Thus, the subsequent liquidator could charge the appointee with trespass on the company's property and claim damages therefor. Acceptance of the appointment may be given orally or in writing. If given orally (e.g. if time is short) the AR must give written confirmation of acceptance to the appointer within seven days.

The Act does not specify any time limits covering the period between the time when the bank makes demand for repayment of the debt and the appointment of the AR. Usually the time lapse is minimal. In *Cripps (Pharmaceuticals) Ltd* v *Wickenden* (1973) a period of approximately one hour was held to be sufficient.

Duties of the administrative receiver

The duties of the AR may be summarised as follows:

(1) The AR must give notice of his appointment to the Registrar of Companies within seven days of appointment. In addition, he must advertise his appointment in the *London Gazette* and a suitable local newspaper.

(2) The AR does not act for the unsecured creditors or agree claims. He does however owe such creditors a fiduciary duty in respect of maximising realisations and thus preserving the company estate for them.

(3) The AR may have any petition for an administration order dismissed (see Chapter 13).

(4) The AR must give notice of his appointment to the company and within 28 days of appointment notify his appointment to all the company's creditors of whom he is aware.

(5) Within 28 days (or such longer time as the AR or the court may allow) the AR must receive a statement of affairs from the company.

(6) Within three months of appointment the AR must send to the Registrar of Companies, to any trustee for the debenture holders and to all creditors (including the bank) a full report of all events leading to his appointment, any disposals of property he intends to follow and the likely proceeds. Such report must also be laid before a creditors' meeting held with 14 days' notice.

(7) A creditors' committee, which has no real powers, may be constituted at a creditors' meeting.

Powers of the administrative receiver

The powers of the AR are extensive and equate to those of the administrator (see Chapter 13). Schedule 1 of the Act enumerates these powers, which give the AR sufficient scope to manage and run the company.

The AR is the agent of the company, which is then responsible for his acts and defaults. Nevertheless he is liable for his own contracts and will often require a specific indemnity from the company (or his appointer) to cover acts for which he may be found liable, e.g. a misfeasance within his remit to the company or breach of fiduciary duty to the company (s. 212 of the Act). Although the directors of the company are not automatically dismissed when the AR appears, their powers to deal with the company's property are suspended during the receivership.

The remuneration of the AR is normally fixed by the appointers. Where the AR is appointed by the trustees of debenture holders, the appointment will be made by the court to which the AR is responsible. It may happen that an unsatisfied creditor or creditors will initiate winding up proceedings through the court during the receivership. Indeed, the creditors may press for a creditors' voluntary winding up at that time. However, the advent of winding up will not affect the AR's position to any great extent, e.g. he may still realise the assets of the company under his charge. The AR is no longer the agent of the company. He cannot continue trading and there is a possibility that his 'charge' may be voided as a preference. The mere fact that liquidation has commenced does not affect the safety of the debenture holder's security.

Practical considerations

A number of practical considerations must be taken into account by the bank which appoints the AR, and indeed the AR himself, as to the viability of the AR route in any given situation. For example, in respect of the financial situation of the company and the outstanding loans:

- Are the loans *intra vires* the company's statutes?

- Has the floating charge been properly registered and could it be held to be a 'preference' if created within the past six months? Moreover, if it was created within the past 12 months was the company solvent at the time? If it was not solvent the charge may be void.

- Is there an administrator appointed and, if so, was he properly appointed?

Also, when the whole question of the company continuing to trade as a worthwhile practical proposition is considered:

- Is there a substantial measure of goodwill which may in time be realisable?

- If there are substantial amounts of raw materials available or work in progress maybe the company should 'trade them out to completion' to obtain the cash benefits.

- There may be adverse factors such as a preponderance of materials held on reservation of title basis, lack of proper space or equipment to trade or a growing lack of confidence amongst the company's customers or suppliers.

Every aspect of the company must be taken into account before the decision is made to appoint an AR. Perhaps the bank will wait until it has reason to suppose the company's debts are at a low ebb (the bank account may assist here) and then act with speed, i.e. appoint an AR within an hour. Timing is crucial in all insolvency work, as is judgment and skill on the part of those involved.

CHAPTER THIRTEEN

The administration order

Definition

Prior to 1986 the ailing company had little practical chance of continuing to trade unless formal receivership was instituted. The advent of the AR was dependent upon the existence of a creditor who was secured by a floating charge over all (or most) of the company's assets and who was willing to initiate proceedings. The unsecured creditors had little choice but to wait in hope of repayment of their debts by the company or else press for liquidation. Winding up was not always the best answer by any means, as will be discussed later in this chapter. There was thus a kind of limbo for the majority of creditors. This matter was addressed by the Cork Committee. It should be pointed out that the Companies Act 1985 s. 425 provides a scheme which could meet the situation given above. This is nothing new in that s. 425 was a carry over from s. 206 of the Companies Act 1948. However, it is generally recognised that the s. 425 scheme, which enables the court to approve a reconstruction of a company which is binding on all creditors, is full of both practical and theoretical difficulties and as a result it is seldom used these days.

The limbo referred to above has been addressed in the Act by the provision of the administration order, which is a new concept to IPs in the United Kingdom. The Act s. 8 (2) defines the administration order as follows:

> An administration order is an order directing that, during the period for which the order is in force, the affairs, business and property of the company shall be managed by a person (the administrator) appointed for the purpose by the court.

The above definition of an administration order may be contrasted with that for an AR (i.e. a receivership) given above. The powers of the AR and the administrator are very similar. The crucial differences between the two procedures (administration and administrative receivership) lie in the methods of appointment and the circumstances surrounding each appointment. Thus, the AR is appointed by a secured creditor having a floating charge on the debtor company's assets and containing powers to make such an appointment. The administrator is appointed by the court hearing a petition for such appointment presented by the company itself, the directors or by a creditor or creditors. In effect the unsecured creditors or the directors of an insolvent company have a similar choice to that of the secured creditor (having a floating charge on the company's assets) in reviving an ailing company and hopefully avoiding the eventual compulsory liquidation of the company. The details of both these procedures are covered in Chapter 12 and in this chapter. The question of the floating charge over the assets of a debtor company (or some of such assets) is covered in Chapter 15.

The administration order, which some say bears likeness to the provisions of Chapter 11 of the US Bankruptcy Code, is an order of court whereby an IP (who is known as the administrator) takes control of the company. He will examine the entire financial situation and the general trading circumstances of the company. He produces proposals for an arrangement with the creditors for the preservation of the company as an ongoing business or at least for maximising the asset base of the company in the event of subsequent liquidation.

Practical emphasis of the administration order

The general emphasis of the administration order lies in the fact that during the currency of the order the control of the company is in the hands of an independent expert. There is a strong element (perhaps) of damage limitation in that incompetent or careless directors cannot cause even more harm to the company's fortunes. The administrator takes steps to stop the rot. The interests of the creditors are (perhaps for the first time) given their true degree of importance and priority. During the period of the administration order, creditors are precluded from taking precipitate action which could damage the overall strength of the business by piecemeal realisation of assets secured by them.

The creditors as a body all share in the independent approach of the administrator. Even if the trading position of the business is seemingly hopeless the administrator, who often acts swiftly and decisively, can at least lessen the ultimate loss to the creditors. It may not follow that the administration order is the answer to the creditors' prayers. Much will depend on the skill and determination of the administrator and the willingness of creditors to co-operate in full at the outset (especially the secured creditors). The existence of a creditor secured by a floating charge is crucial (this matter is examined in depth later in this chapter). Unhappily, there are cases where the question of an administration order is aborted at the outset by the simple realisation that immediate liquidation is the only viable route to take in the interests of the creditors. This vehicle for solving the difficulties of the corporate body has been generally welcomed by the business community since 1986 although it seems that criticism has been raised in several quarters as to the fairness of this procedure with regard to the various classes of creditor.

Procedure

The life of the administration order is specified in the Act ss. 8–27 inclusive and in number 2 of the Insolvency Rules.

Section 8(3) specifies the purposes for which an administration order can be made. These include:

(a) the survival of the company, and the whole or any part of its undertaking, as a going concern;

(b) the approval of a voluntary arrangement under Part 1 [the provisions of the CVA];

(c) the sanctioning under s. 425 of the Companies Act [1985] of a compromise or arrangement between the company and any such persons as are mentioned in that section [e.g. the creditors]; and

(d) a more advantageous realisation of the company's assets than would be effected on a winding up.

The court must be satisfied that one (or more) of the above objects are capable of achievement within the scope of the administration order proposed.

Under s. 8 (4) of the Act no company can be put into administration once a winding up order has been made. The court must be satisfied on making an administration order that the company is or is likely to become unable to pay its debts. Salient points covering the administration order are discussed below.

The application for an order

The petition for an administration order may be made to the court by one (or more) of several persons:

● The company itself.

● The directors (as a board; one director can in fact present the petition but only as a result of a board resolution; *Re Equiticorp Int plc* (1989)).

● A creditor or creditors (including any contingent or prospective creditor or creditors; the Act s. 9 (1)).

In addition, the petition must state the name of the proposed administrator (such person being a qualified IP). The petition must be supported by an affidavit and by the consent of the proposed administrator to act as such if the petition is granted by court and an order made (Insolvency Rules number 2.4).

The petition and affidavit are filed at the appropriate court (i.e. the one which has jurisdiction to wind the company up) and the court fixes the date for the hearing. It is then the duty of the petitioner to inform the court in writing of any later winding up petition which may be served against the company immediately on becoming aware of it (Insolvency Rules number 2.5) (4). It is thus possible for the court to hear two petitions at the same time: one for the administration order and one for winding up. In this case the court may choose to grant one petition or, perhaps unlikely, refuse both.

The Act s. 9 (2) indicates those persons who must receive copies of the petition. These include:

● the person who has appointed, or is or may be entitled to appoint, an AR of the company and to such other persons as may be prescribed (those persons are listed in the Insolvency Rules 1986 number 2.6 (2));

● if there is a pending petition for winding up then on that petitioner and also on the company's provisional liquidator, if there is one. A copy must also be served on the person proposed as administrator. If the petitioner(s) is/are creditor(s) of the company then a copy must also be served on the company.

The crucial point here is that those who are affected by an administration order being made against a company are made aware of the position at the outset. Apart from the matter of the company already being under attack from a winding up petition, the holder of a floating charge (e.g. the company's bank lending against a debenture) is made aware of the petition for an administration order in time to take evasive action if necessary. As will be discussed later in this chapter, a banker may through an AR utilise his rights to oppose the administration order. Incidentally, copies of the petition must be served not less than five days before the hearing date.

The effect of the petition

Section 10 of the Act states that between the dates on which the petition is filed at court and the hearing date:

● no resolution may be passed or order made for the winding up of the company;

● no steps may be taken by creditor(s) to enforce any security in their hands;

● no other proceedings and no execution or other legal process may be commenced or continued against the company being petitioned without leave of the court.

Thus the moratorium effect of the administration order begins when the petition is filed in court. This point is vital to all creditors of the company. The advertisement of the petition signifies to the market that the company is in deep trouble. Section 10 of the Act continues with instructions which may well provide important avenues for some creditors, e.g. the banker secured by a floating charge, to explore.

It appears that leave of court is not required during the period between the lodging of the petition and the hearing for the presentation of a winding up petition (which would then be heard concurrently with the one for the administration order as has already been explained). Also, where a petition for an administration order is presented at a time when there is an AR of the company and the person by whom or on whose behalf the receiver was appointed has not consented to the making of the order, then the period mentioned in subsection (1) (from petition to order) does not commence until that person so consents.

The holder of a floating charge can appoint an AR (if one has not already been appointed) and thus block the administration order. It is assumed that the floating charge clause within the debenture deed is such that the lodging of a petition for an administration order is taken to be an event of default under the terms of the debenture and in turn that clause is tied to an event of default clause entitling the debenture holder, the lending bank, to appoint an AR.

It must be emphasised that the 'moratorium effect' of the administration order is crucial to the (possible) survival of the company and the general position of the creditors. The section below entitled 'the effect of the order' illustrates in practical terms the extent to which the moratorium situation applies with regard to the general commercial dealings of the company.

The hearing

The court may make an administration order on hearing the petition provided it is satisfied that one or more of the statutory objectives of the administration order (mentioned above) are achievable. Alternatively, the court may adjourn the hearing, make an interim order if appropriate or make any other suitable order. The court has, in effect, a free hand to act as it sees fit. The adjournment option is available partly because the short time span between the lodging of the petition and the hearing may be insufficient for all parties to complete their pleas to court.

The effect of the order

If the court makes an administration order at the hearing then the die is cast so to speak. The Act s. 11 (and other sections) makes a number of rules which must now be activated. These include, on the making of the order:

- Any outstanding petition for winding up is dismissed.
- Any AR in place shall vacate office. (This assumes the AR did not object to the order.)

⬤ Any receiver appointed under the Law of Property Act 1925 by a secured creditor over property of the company shall vacate office if required to do so by the administrator. (It seems this is not automatic since the administrator has a choice of action here.)

⬤ No resolution for winding up can be passed (e.g. as a creditors' voluntary winding up).

⬤ No AR can be appointed.

⬤ No other steps may be taken by creditors to enforce or realise their security and no other action to effect recovery or enforce repayment of debts may be taken by creditors without the consent of the court or the administrator.

It may be seen that the secured creditor does not lose his security as such. He does, however, lose his ability to realise that security without the agreement of the court or the administrator to proceed with the sale. The banker who holds a floating charge over the undertaking of the company does in effect lose control over events in that the administrator takes control of the company, thus depriving the floating chargee of much of his power over the situation. The law recognises this in that the floating chargee has, as already described, the ability to avoid the administration order. It is questionable whether this rule will remain on the statute book for much longer.

Once the administration order is made the administrator must publicise it in the prescribed manner, i.e. in the *London Gazette*, notice to the companies registry, to floating chargees, any person who has presented a winding up petition and the company. In addition, the administrator must notify all known creditors within 28 days of the order. Finally, all company notepaper and invoices, etc. must show the administrator's name.

The administrator

The Act ss. 14 *et seq.* and the Rules provide a framework giving the powers and duties of the administrator. His powers are necessarily extensive. Indeed, s. 14 (1) of the Act states:

The administrator of a company

(a) may do all such things as may be necessary for the management of the affairs, business and property of the company . . . and

(b) without prejudice to the generality of paragraph (a) has powers specified in Schedule 1 to the Act.

Schedule 1 of the Act entitled 'Powers of administrator or administrative receiver' includes some 23 clauses giving the administrator diverse, almost unlimited, powers over the company's affairs. The administrator, who is the company's agent, has the power to remove any director and appoint an alternative if necessary. He can also call meetings of shareholders or creditors and he may apply to court for direction on any matter concerning the carrying out of his functions.

Secured creditors will note that the administrator has, by virtue of s. 15 of the Act, the power to dispose of company property which is subject to charge in favour of a creditor. The administrator must first obtain the permission of the court and assure the court that the sale of such asset(s) will contribute towards attaining one of the objectives set out in the petition. Of interest is s. 15(5) of the Act, which provides that the net proceeds of disposal of the asset in question shall be used in discharging the debt upon which such asset was security. Section 15(5)(b) states:

> where those proceeds are less than such amount as may be determined by the court to be the net amount which would be realised on a sale of the property or goods in the open market by a willing vendor, such sums as may be required to make good the deficiency shall be applied towards discharging the sums secured by the security.

The above statement brings to mind a famous retort heard on the tennis court: 'You cannot be serious'. If the clause is not a drafting error, the effect seems to be that where the administrator undersells a property which is subject to a creditor's charge then he, the administrator, must make good the deficiency in sale proceeds to the creditor. At least this emphasises the heavy responsibility the administrator has in correctly fulfilling his functions in managing the company.

The administrator's fees are fixed by the court within the guidelines in the Rules number 2.47. The remuneration figure is set in accordance with a fixed percentage of value in property handled or simply based on time costs to the administrator and his staff. The complexity of the case and any exceptional responsibilities undertaken, etc. would be taken into account. Where a committee of creditors is formed, they – and not the court – may fix the sum in question.

The administrator will normally continue the administration order until it is finally lifted, although he can be removed by the court in exceptional cases. He may resign on grounds of ill health, conflict of interest or on ceasing to be an IP. Death is clearly a reason for a new administrator to be appointed.

Specific duties and liabilities of the administrator

The rules referred to above lay down some specific routine actions for the administrator to follow. For example:

● The administrator must obtain from present and past officers of the company and present and past (up to one year maximum) staff a full statement of the affairs of the company. Particulars such as assets, debts, securities given, etc. must be included in the statement.

● Within three months of the order, the administrator must formulate his proposals, which are then sent to the Registrar of Companies, all creditors (of whom he is aware) and all members. The document sent to the Registrar of Companies (and which is laid before the creditors' meeting) must be full and give the creditors opportunity to assess the position of the company.

● A point of contention for some time past has been the extent to which an administrator (or AR) has been liable to cover employees' contracts in cases where he had not dismissed company staff. In 1985 the courts ruled, in the case *Nicoll* v *Cutts*, in favour of the receivers and against a director who had sued them claiming he was entitled to compensation because he had not formally been dismissed. Up until that time receivers had simply paid employees during the period during which they (the receivers) were in charge of the company. The 1986 Act changed the ruling and stated that administrators and receivers would be liable after 14 days after appointment for all outstanding employment obligations including long-term service contracts of the directors. This rule was tested in 1987 through a case, *Re Specialised Mouldings*, which supported actions taken by receivers, in that they were not deemed to have adopted employees' contracts where they had written to staff informing them that they were not adopting their contracts. The temptation was then for administrators or receivers to lay off staff rather than risk substantial additional obligations and become personally liable for any shortfall, thus prejudicing any rescue (particularly in case of labour intensive companies). The situation related above has serious overtones. As the Act stood when the case *Powdrill and Another* v *Watson and Another* (1994) (the *Paramount Airways* case) was heard on appeal at the end of February 1994, it appeared likely that administrators or receivers would shut companies down or put them into liquidation within 13 days of appointment rather than help them trade out their problems. The risk to the IP of running a business for 14 days or more and becoming liable for all contracts of employment and being open to legal action by creditors who appointed him, was too great (albeit the IP had the usual indemnities). Receivers and administrators could have had to find cash from their own resources if the company had inadequate funds with which to pay claims on employment contracts. It has been said that one consequence of putting employees at the top of the creditor list is that a director with a five year contract would scoop the pool, yet he might have got the company into the mess in the first place.

The whole topic of employees' contracts was the subject of intense lobbying by the insolvency profession in the two weeks following the *Paramount Airways* decision. This resulted in Parliament passing the Insolvency Act 1994, which received the royal assent on 24 March 1994 and applies to all contracts of employment adopted on or after 15 March of that year. This Act amends *inter alia* s. 19 of the Insolvency Act 1986 in that employment contracts adopted by administrators or receivers after 15 March 1994 attract liability towards them only with regard to services rendered by employees after the adoption of the contract. This appears to solve the dilemma and effectively puts the position back to what it was before 1986. It is good news for jobs and gives back to administrators the opportunity to manage companies back into solvency.

● The administrator must send the documentation described with the agenda and proxy form to all known creditors within three months of the administration order. The creditors must have 21 days' notice of the meeting, as specified in the agenda.

● Voting at the creditors' meeting must be by majority in value of votes cast in person or by proxy. The rules in general are similar to those for a creditors' meeting summoned in connection with a CVA as discussed in Chapter 11. The result of the meeting must be sent to all known creditors, the Registrar of Companies and the court within 14 days of the meeting. If the meeting approves the administrator's proposals then such findings can only be amended subsequently with the approval of a further creditors' meeting. If it transpires that the creditors cannot agree the administrator's plans (i.e. by the requisite majority), the court may discharge the order and substitute another.

● If the creditors approve the scheme put forward by the administrator they may form a creditors' committee. This will consist of between three and five elected creditors who will assist the administrator in his duties and collect updated information from him on the progress of the matter. In any case, the administrator is bound to send an abstract of receipts and payments after every six months to the court, the Registrar of Companies and members of any creditors' committee.

● As and when the whole administration can be concluded (i.e. when the purpose of the administration order has been fulfilled) or if the administrator feels that the purpose is incapable of being fulfilled, or the creditors require him to do so, an application to court is made by the administrator for the order to be discharged. The court can at this stage if necessary make a winding up order.

Directors and secretary

The powers of the directors of a company which has gone into administration in general are subordinated to those of the administrator as is the position of the secretary. The Act s. 14 (2) states:

> the administrator has powers to remove any director of the company and to appoint any person to be a director of it whether to fill a vacancy or otherwise.

Furthermore, s. 14 (4) states:

> any power conferred on the company or its officers [e.g. the secretary] whether by this Act or the Companies Act or by the Memorandum or Articles which could be exercised in such a way as to interfere with the exercise by the administrator of his powers is not exercisable except with the consent of the Administrator, which may be given generally or in relation to particular cases.

It thus seems that the powers of the administrator are supreme.

It is true that under s. 27 of the Act creditors and/or members may apply to court for an order to regulate the future management by the administrator of the company's affairs, business and property on the grounds of unfair prejudice. However the directors cannot themselves make such application solely in their capacity as director (or as secretary). The position of directors may be unsatisfactory in that they still have statutory duties under the Companies Act 1985 with regard to the filing of accounts and returns to Companies House and to keeping statutory records. Clearly a degree of co-operation between the directors and the administrator (if the directors are retained) is called for and in any case the administrator can always apply to court for direction on this (or any other) issue concerning the administration under the terms of the Act s. 14 (3).

Practical considerations

Viability of the administration order

The viability of the administration order can be difficult to evaluate in relation to one or more of the statutory and specified objectives. The bigger the company, the more complicated the trading position, the more desperate the cash flow position and the more creditors who are secured, then the more difficult is the decision as to whether to accept the administrator's proposals for the creditors. The various parties concerned, that is the creditors, employees, shareholders and secured and unsecured creditors may all look at the position from different angles – and understandably so. The general philosophy behind the administration order was outlined at the beginning of this chapter. It may be helpful at this point to examine the many practical considerations (or at least some of the more important ones).

Size of the business

Where the business is not so large that it presents the administrator with an awesome task and the balance sheet and profit and loss figures give at least a measure of hope the administration order could be a good solution. Assuming that none of the creditors are secured by a floating charge on the undertaking, e.g. the company's bankers, and indeed no more than a reasonable portion of the company's assets are secured to creditors, it could be assumed that the creditors will listen sympathetically to any sensible proposal for the administration order. It may be that a voluntary arrangement is seen as a good alternative route but the immediate (temporary) moratorium on hostile attacks from creditors, which could upset the delicate equilibrium of the company's finances, is necessary as a first step. A look at the asset side of the company's balance sheet (or rather the statement of affairs) may reveal some powerful considerations to be taken into account by the creditors. Creditors who have sold raw materials, etc. to the company under 'reservation of title' (ROT) contracts may feel that the administration would be to their benefit (see page 171). The continued trading of the company to the point where the ROT debts are cleared may well be preferable to an ROT claim against a liquidator in due course.

Overseas assets

The existence of company assets in a foreign jurisdiction can often be a major problem for the administrator or liquidator. Questions regarding conflict of laws and jurisdictional matters as well as the expenses and delays incurred in instituting actions in an overseas court may dampen the enthusiasm of the creditors for liquidation. At least the administrator or liquidator will have a court appointment and thus an 'official' status in an overseas court where sometimes only a court order is recognised as providing sufficient authority to the holder to plead in that court.

Accounting matters

It may be that accounting considerations of the company alone will dictate the answer to the company's problems. The administration route may well allow the administrator to let the business run down as smoothly as possible and to choose the time and decide on the need to realise assets. The going concern picture on the balance sheet may be vastly different from the true picture since many of the assets, e.g. work in progress, may be realisable at a pittance if not at a loss.

Presence of a debenture holder

There may well be circumstances when an administration order would be totally inappropriate. If a bank is holding a fixed and floating charge on the assets side of the balance sheet (in whatever form – the so called 'all monies' debenture is extremely sophisticated), this may well be sufficient to cause the creditors to abandon any possibility of an administration order. Even if the bank allows the order, the structure of the security interests in favour of the lending bank may well render any administration order unworkable. Indeed, the court might turn down the idea anyway. Questions of cost must always be taken into account. The liquidator's fees and expenses (often considerable) may still work out cheaper in the long run than the costs of an administrator in a protracted administration. There is currently no stated time limit on the overall length of an administration order. Admittedly, periodic reports must be filed by the administrator, as has been explained, but even so the best answer may be a liquidation whereby the creditors cut their losses and get what they can from the wreck as soon as possible.

Creditors' position

In the final analysis the fact that the administrator must make an in-depth feasibility study of the company's fortunes is crucial. The court will have to be convinced as to the viability of any scheme and it may be that the creditors are the least of the administrator's problems. The administration order is no easy option for the insolvent company and it is the creditors' position which must take primary consideration. The directors of the company considering an administration order must of course be conscious that if the company is in fact insolvent or in serious trouble they are duty bound to do whatever they can to alleviate the company's position. The twin clouds of wrongful and fraudulent trading hang over them (in practice the former only in most cases). Clearly, if a director is innocent of any wrongdoing he has little to fear other than the disruption to his personal life caused by the company scenario. Admittedly this is traumatic enough but he is better placed than a director who stands liable to be called to account for his past misdeeds. Any director who has reason to fear for the company's financial well-being must surely seek professional advice in addition to discussing the matter with his co-directors and shareholders.

Bankers' position

Bankers may see the matter of the administration order from a different angle from other creditors. Where the company's account is in credit (or is a fully secured debt) then there is no immediate cause for concern. The advent of an administrator would be a turning point in the banker–customer relationship. Of immediate concern in cases where the bank has a floating charge on the undertaking of the company – as already mentioned – is that the bank must decide whether or not to oppose the order and thus appoint an AR. Where an LPA receiver has been appointed over a property under charge to the bank, further considerations may apply. The administrator, if appointed, may require the receiver to go. One can conceive of circumstances where the lending banker may welcome – or even initiate – a petition for an administration order. Thus, the bank's debt may be comparatively small compared to the asset base of the company. The bank may be unsecured and welcome the advent of a professional IP to take control of (possibly) troublesome and uncooperative directors.

The bank could be unsure as to how far it can go in advising an ailing company by reason of the danger of becoming a 'shadow director' with all that entails (see page 188). The 1990 case of *M C Bacon* highlights this concern. Putting a company's affairs into the hands of an administrator may come as a welcome relief to the hard pressed bank manager. In addition, as has already been mentioned, where a company has significant assets in a foreign jurisdiction the administration order may be useful. The bank must consider the plus and minus points as must all the other parties involved.

The bank has a distinct advantage in that it almost certainly has a lot more information to assist it in reaching a decision than most trade creditors, whose information may be too sparse to enable them to reach an effective decision. Until such creditors receive the proposals and statement of affairs they may be completely ignorant of their chances of ultimate repayment. One interesting dilemma the bank could face is that if it appoints an AR (assuming it is in a position to do so) it could precipitate the downfall of the company, a situation which might otherwise have been avoided. If the bank does not appoint an AR it will lose the right to do so anyway once the administrator is appointed. (This assumes that the lending bank is not already adequately secured with legal charges over the company's assets).

The creditors' position can be judged by consideration of the rules covered in this chapter. Often the creditors must welcome the administration order. At least it indicates that something is happening. Presumably any creditor who sees the majority of others vote for the order must have a powerful reason for deciding to vote against the proposal. The secured creditor may be almost indifferent to the possibility of the administration order.

When considering an administration order as an alternative to liquidation (or at least as a delaying tactic) many factors have to be taken into account. However, the administration order agrees with the general underlying philosophy of the recent insolvency legislation in that the debtor is provided with a route which, if applicable and agreeable to the creditors, may enable liquidation to be avoided, thus preserving the business, if not the company as well. Creditors may well suffer less than they might have done under the pre-1986 legislation. Changes in the way the administration order is set up and managed are to be expected but in today's business climate the administration order system is an option worthy of consideration.

CHAPTER FOURTEEN

Corporate winding up

As mentioned in Chapter 10 there are currently two types of winding up procedure which a limited company may adopt. These are:

● the voluntary liquidation, i.e. the members' voluntary liquidation or the creditors' voluntary liquidation;

● the compulsory liquidation.

The various circumstances which may lead a company to choose one of the above will now be analysed and the procedures applicable to each type of winding up will be examined.

The members' voluntary liquidation

As indicated above, there are two types of voluntary liquidation. If the company's directors are able to swear a declaration of solvency (see below) the winding up will be by way of a members' voluntary liquidation. Strictly speaking this type of liquidation is not an insolvency procedure at all since all creditors will be paid in full. However, it is necessary to appreciate the reasons for this route to be adopted by a company and how it is put into effect to gain a complete picture of the winding up of a corporate entity in all its forms.

Circumstances when a members' voluntary liquidation is used

Section 84 of the Act gives the circumstances in which a company may be wound up voluntarily. These include:

(a) when the period (if any) fixed for the duration of the company by the articles expires, or an event (if any) occurs, on the occurrence of which the articles provide that the company is to be dissolved, and the company in general meeting had passed a resolution requiring it to be wound up voluntarily;

(b) if the company resolves by special resolution that it be wound up voluntarily;

(c) if the company resolves by extraordinary resolution to the effect that it cannot by reason of its liabilities continue in business, and that it is advisable to wind up.

There are thus a number of cogent reasons why a company may be obliged to take the members' voluntary liquidation route. The business may be making losses and prudence may demand that liquidation takes place before insolvency becomes apparent thereby leaving the shareholders with little or no return on their capital. It may well be that the purpose of the company has been achieved and the articles may make it clear that when such purpose has been met winding up must ensue. Then again, it sometimes happens that the shareholders become estranged and are unable to agree on future plans and strategies of the company. A further reason for a members' voluntary liquidation may arise in cases where the shareholders wish to sell the business but find that no buyer wants to purchase the business as one whole unit. Therefore a liquidation and sell off of component parts of the business will achieve the desired result.

Company solvency

A crucial aspect of a members' voluntary liquidation is that the company is solvent at the commencement of the winding up and remains so until the company name is eventually taken off the register of companies.

The members' voluntary winding up is basically a director led process. The conduct and efficacy of the liquidation is propelled by the board and the court is not involved. There are minimal statutory costs involved in the entire procedure. The creditors have no say with regard to the manner in which the liquidator proceeds.

The procedure to be adopted in the members' voluntary liquidation

The Act ss. 84–96 give the various points to note in respect of the procedure to be adopted in a members' voluntary winding up. The stages in the process are listed below.

The declaration of solvency

The directors (or at least a majority of them) must make a statutory declaration pursuant to the terms of the Act s. 89 that after full enquiry they are of the opinion that the company will be able to pay its debts plus interest within a period of 12 months from the commencement of the winding up. Such declaration made at a directors' meeting must be made within five weeks preceding the date of the passing of the resolution for winding up and have attached a statement of the company's assets and liabilities made shortly before the declaration. Furthermore, the list of assets must show a realisable value which may not be exactly the same as the value shown on the last balance sheet. Such declaration must be delivered to the Registrar of Companies within 15 days after the resolution is passed, and any director(s) making a false declaration is liable to a fine or imprisonment or both. Should more than five weeks elapse between the making of the declaration and the members' meeting called to vote on a winding up resolution then the declaration lapses. The directors could at this point make another declaration and start the proceedings afresh.

Problems may arise for a director in cases where, after the director has made the statutory declaration it transpires that the company's debts are not settled or provided for within the time limit of 12 months from commencement of winding up. The Act s. 89 (5) states that in these circumstances the director concerned is 'presumed [unless the contrary is shown] not to have had reasonable grounds for his opinion'. This may be one of the few instances where the law presumes an accused person to be guilty unless he proves innocence. If the liquidator finds that the company has little chance of paying its debts within the period laid down in the declaration of solvency he will automatically have the winding up converted to a creditors' voluntary liquidation with the possibility of criminal proceedings being taken against the directors.

The winding up resolution

A meeting of members is then called to consider a resolution for the winding up of the company by means of a members' voluntary liquidation. The articles of the company may govern the requisite voting majority for a winding up resolution. Thus, if no dividends have been paid on preference shares for a specified period the preference shareholders may be allowed to cast votes in this instance. Shareholders must be given at least 21 days' notice of the meeting. A majority for the resolution consisting of 75% of votes cast (in person or by proxy) must be achieved although a majority of shareholders holding at least 95% of the voting rights may agree to shorter notice. A bare majority of votes cast is insufficient.

Once the resolution is passed for a members' voluntary winding up the liquidation commences from that date. A copy of such resolution must be sent to the Registrar of Companies within 15 days and it must be advertised in the *London Gazette* within 14 days. In addition, the following consequences of the resolution take immediate effect under ss. 86–88 of the Act:

(1) The business of the company ceases except that which is necessary for the winding up.

(2) The corporate state and powers of the company continue until dissolution.

(3) Any transfer of the company's shares is void without the liquidator's consent.

(4) Any change in the status of the shareholders is void.

Appointment of the liquidator

The appointment of the liquidator, who must be an IP, is made at the meeting of members described above at which the winding up resolution is passed. His fees are usually fixed at the same time. The liquidator derives his authority from the chairman's written statement presented at the meeting. In addition, he must send notice of his appointment to all creditors within 28 days. Although it is unusual in the case of a members' voluntary liquidation a special manager may also be appointed to manage the company's business or property where such management calls for particular specialised skills.

Progress of the winding up

Since the company is fully solvent in a members' voluntary liquidation there should be few problems regarding the sale and disposal of assets and the settlement of all debts by the company. The routine aspects of progress such as proof of debts, secured creditors, disclaimers of onerous property, liquidator's statements to the Registrar of

Companies, etc. are similar to those pertaining to the creditors' voluntary winding up, which will be covered later in this chapter. However, questions regarding the apportionment of assets to separate classes of creditor will clearly not apply. There is no Value Added Tax (VAT) bad debt relief applicable here since all creditors will be paid in full plus VAT. There will be no creditors' committee since (again) this will hardly be necessary. The liquidator will pay careful attention to the terms of the company's Articles on the rights of various classes of shareholders, e.g. it may be that where preference shares are in issue, members will be entitled to participate in any surplus once a certain minimum has been paid on the ordinary shares.

Completion of the winding up

Once the affairs of the company are wound up, the liquidator calls a final meeting of members and lays before it a final account giving details of the liquidation. Within a week after the meeting he sends to the Registrar of Companies a copy of the final accounts and confirmation of the meeting. The Registrar will then strike the company's name off the register of companies three months after receiving the documentation (s. 201 of the Act).

As already mentioned, if at any time the liquidator forms the opinion that the company is in reality insolvent he will call a meeting of creditors of the company within 28 days of such discovery and take steps to have the winding up continued as a creditors' voluntary liquidation.

The creditors' voluntary liquidation

The need for liquidation

Once it becomes apparent to the members and directors of a company that the business is – or is about to become – insolvent then urgent action is advisable. One reason for this is to obviate 'wrongful trading' accusations. The general trading position of the company must be examined closely and note taken that at least staff must be paid and suppliers of essential services (such as electricity) must continue to be paid or else such services may be withdrawn. Any adverse publicity in the market may cause suppliers to discontinue deliveries until outstanding arrears are paid and customers may well look elsewhere for future purchases.

The directors' approach

Company directors should be well aware that inaction on their part could lead to charges of wrongful (or fraudulent) trading being made against them if and when liquidation ensues. Every possible step should be taken to minimise potential losses to creditors in order to avoid or alleviate this possibility. To continue to trade without considering the position of creditors whilst knowing that insolvency is near or already a fact can be fraught with disaster for the board of a company. It may be that even at this eleventh hour remedial action could turn the fortunes of the business round. Thus, it may be possible for funds to be obtained by the sale of surplus assets or the company's bankers could be persuaded to allow or increase existing credit facilities. Although unlikely, shareholders may be persuaded to inject further capital into the business. If these possibilities are inappropriate – or even impossible – alternatives to liquidation in the form of the appointment of a receiver, an administration order or a voluntary arrangement may be viable.

In the absence of a way out of the situation along the lines given above, the winding up of the company is the only alternative. Indeed, the directors will realise that a winding up at the hands of the creditors – known as a creditors' voluntary liquidation – is advisable before a creditor petitions for a compulsory liquidation before the court. Whilst the creditors' voluntary winding up is controlled by the creditors, it follows that the shareholders will have little real say or interest in the liquidation apart from approving the process at the outset.

The procedure to be adopted in the creditors' voluntary liquidation

The Act ss. 97–116 apply to a creditors' voluntary liquidation. The stages in the process are described below.

Meetings of the directors, shareholders and creditors

Whilst the directors will need to meet to convene both shareholders' and creditors' meetings, they will also try to ensure the smooth running of the creditors' voluntary liquidation should the shareholders approve such a resolution. The directors should appoint one of their number to chair the creditors' meeting and also approve the statement of affairs which will be laid before them. Other matters for the attention of the directors at this stage include the appointment of an IP to provide advice and assistance in the period before the liquidation in matters such as the banking arrangements and payments for essential costs and services in the time before the creditors' meeting.

The rules covering the convening of the necessary meetings are given in the Act s. 98 and they appear to allow several alternative timetables. For example:

> The company shall:
>
> (a) cause a meeting of its creditors to be summoned for a day not later than the 14th day after the day on which there is to be held the company meeting at which the resolution for voluntary winding up is to be proposed;
>
> (b) cause the notices of the creditors' meeting to be sent by post to the creditors not less than 7 days before the day on which the meeting is to be held; and
>
> (c) cause notice of the creditors' meeting to be advertised once in the *Gazette* and once at least in two newspapers circulating in the relevant locality (that is to say the locality in which the company's principal place of business in Great Britain was situated during the relevant period).

Furthermore, s. 98 goes on to state that the name and address of a qualified IP who will give creditors free of charge such information as they may reasonably require on the company's affairs must be included in the notice to the meeting. In addition, the notice of the place where the creditors may within two days before the meeting obtain a list of company creditors in full is included in the notice to the meeting.

Various points relate to s. 98 of the Act, subsection (a) uses the words 'not later than the fourteenth day'. The timetable may be eased in so far as short notice may be given by shareholders for their meeting if members holding 95% of the nominal capital so agree. Also, whilst it is not necessary for notice to the creditors' meeting to be issued at the same time as that for the shareholders it is nevertheless often advisable for the notice to the creditors' meeting to be issued before the members' meeting at which the winding up resolution is passed (s. 98 (b) above).

Thus, in summary it appears that the creditors' meeting must be held up to 14 days after the general meeting of the company at which the winding up resolution is passed and that the creditors must have seven days' notice of their meeting. Often the directors will arrange for the two meetings to be held on the same day with the creditors' meeting held immediately after the shareholders' meeting. This is possible if the directors give the shareholders the mandatory 14 days notice and convene the creditors on the same day. Alternatively, the directors may be able to obtain short notice agreement from the members and still give the creditors the statutory seven days notice.

Circumstances may compel the directors to arrange a members' meeting at minimum short notice and to hold a creditors' meeting 14 days thereafter. This alternative may be useful in cases where the complex affairs of the company warrant a maximum period during which to prepare the agenda for the creditors' meeting and the statement of affairs, etc.

The liquidation commences at the date the winding up resolution is passed.

At the meeting of creditors the agenda will include the following:

● The appointment of a liquidator – or joint liquidators – and (possibly) the establishment of the liquidator's remuneration.

● The establishment of a liquidation committee.

● The possibility of adjournment for up to three weeks to consider outstanding matters.

● Any other business as appropriate.

In addition, the statement of affairs will be laid before the meeting and copies – or summaries – of the statement should be handed to creditors before the meeting commences. The director chairing the meeting will usually give the meeting a summary of the company's position and a short history of events leading up to it. Whilst this aspect of the meeting is not laid down in statute, it should be seen as being only fair in order that the creditors present can evaluate the position and come to a correct decision as to whether to appoint a liquidation committee and whom to appoint as liquidator.

The quorum for the meeting consists of one creditor present (or represented by proxy) if the meeting consists of the chairman and one other person and at the same time the chairman is aware that one or more persons would be entitled to vote had they attended (Insolvency Rules 1986 number 12.4). Moreover, voting is to be by majority in value of claims lodged and present in person or by proxy (Insolvency Rules 1986 number 4.63).

The statement of affairs

The Act s. 99 states that the directors shall prepare a statement of affairs, which is to be laid before the creditors' meeting. The statement shall include:

(a) particulars of the company's assets, debts and liabilities;

(b) names and addresses of the company's creditors;

(c) the securities [if any] held by the creditors;

(d) the dates when the securities [in (c) above] were respectively given;

(e) such further or other information as may be prescribed.

Should any director fail without reasonable excuse to comply with the provisions of s. 99 by not completing an adequate statement or not attend the creditors' meeting when appointed to do so by the other directors, then he shall be liable to a fine.

A copy of the statement of affairs (or a summary thereof) and a report of the proceedings at the creditors' meeting must be sent by the liquidator to all contributories within 28 days after the meeting.

Section 100 (2) of the Act states:

The liquidator shall be the person nominated by the creditors or, where no person has been so nominated, the person (if any) nominated by the company.

Where the chairman of the creditors' meeting has the written consent of the person proposed and voted for as liquidator, who must be a qualified IP, to act then the chairman may certify such appointment. The date of the appointment is effectively the date of the resolution of appointment.

The voting for a liquidator by the creditors shall be by majority in value of claims lodged and present in person or by proxy. It may be that the company already has a liquidator in which case the chairman of the creditors' meeting will ascertain whether they have an alternative candidate. If there is no overall majority at the creditors' meeting for one person then the one with least votes drops out and a further vote is taken.

The liquidation

Where the company has appointed a liquidator before the creditors' meeting (but after the resolution to wind up), the liquidator has limited powers. He may take control of and insure company assets and he can only sell assets which are of a perishable nature or are in danger of losing value. Any further actions by him must have prior court approval.

Once the liquidator's appointment is approved by the creditors, the winding up will be advertised in the *London Gazette* and in a local newspaper and the information will be sent to the Registrar of Companies.

The powers and duties of the liquidator are extensive. For example, the liquidator must:

- keep proper books and records of the winding up;

- liaise with a liquidation committee of creditors, if one is formed, and seek their sanction for certain actions as specified in Part I of Schedule 4 of the Act, e.g. pay any class of creditor in full or reach a compromise with the creditors (if there is no liquidation committee then he must obtain court sanction for such acts);

- realise the company's assets and pay dividends to creditors;

- make a report to the DTI within six months of the commencement of the liquidation if he considers that any person who was a director (or a shadow director) of the company at any time within three years prior to the commencement of the winding up is unfit to manage a company (Company Directors Disqualification Act 1986 s. 7(3)); proceedings may of course be taken against any director being reported on and the penalties of the Act may be imposed;

- file detailed statements of progress in the winding up at six monthly intervals with the Registrar of Companies;

- conduct annual meetings with the creditors and shareholders and inform the meetings in detail as to progress with the liquidation.

Once the liquidation is completed the liquidator will call final meetings and resign. A copy of the final accounts and details of the final meetings will be sent to the Registrar of Companies and after three months the company will be struck off the company register of names.

The compulsory liquidation

The compulsory liquidation of a company is designed to achieve the same purpose as a voluntary winding up, namely the dissolution of the company. Creditors must be paid rateably within each class and any surplus goes to the shareholders (with a members' voluntary winding up of course the shareholders are repaid in full). However, the compulsory liquidation is significant in that the proceedings are driven by the court and the liquidator is acting as an officer of the court.

The High Court can wind up any company although where a company's paid-up share capital does not exceed £120 000 the County

Court of the district where the company has its registered office has concurrent jurisdiction to wind up the company. However, proceedings commenced in the wrong court are not invalid (ss. 117 and 118).

Circumstances requiring court intervention

The fact that a company is wound up by the court does not necessarily signify that such company is insolvent although that is so in most cases. The Act s. 122 specifies the circumstances in which the company may be wound up by the court when:

(a) the company has by special resolution resolved that it be wound up by the court;

(b) being a public company which was registered as such on its original incorporation, the company has not been issued with a certificate under section 117 of the Companies Act (public company share capital requirements) and more than a year has expired since it was so registered;

(c) the company is an old public company within the meaning of the Companies Consolidation (Consequential Provisions) Act 1985 section 1;

(d) the company does not commence business within one year of incorporation or suspends its business for a whole year;

(e) the number of members is reduced below two;

(f) the company is unable to pay its debts;

(g) the court is of the opinion that it is just and equitable that the company should be wound up.

Two points should be mentioned regarding the above. Firstly, in respect of (e) above, the Companies (Single Member Private Limited Companies) Regulations 1992 (SI 1992/1699) came into force on 15 July 1992 as a result of European Directive No 89/667/EEC. This SI abolished the somewhat artificial situation where a business proprietor is in reality a sole owner of a business but has his spouse (or any other close partner) to hold one share to accommodate the previous 'two member' rule. Even so, the new regulations still make it necessary for a company having one member (assuming the Articles allow this) to have another officer of the company as secretary. The 1992 Regulations in appropriate circumstances override the Act in this matter. Secondly, whereas point (g) above is often pleaded as an alternative in a petition under one of the other headings, e.g. (f), it can be successfully used on its own in circumstances where:

● the company is in effect a quasi-partnership and relations between the partners have broken down (*Re Yenidje Tobacco Co Ltd* (1916));

● the affairs of the company are being improperly conducted;

● the company is in reality conducting fraudulent business or has been fraudulently formed;

● a company has been formed to achieve a purpose which it becomes clear is incapable of being met by the company.

However, it is with situations where the company is unable to pay its debts that the impact of insolvency law is most concerned.

Inability of the company to pay its debts

The question of exactly what is 'inability to pay debts' has already been discussed (see Chapter 2). So far as the limited company is concerned the Act s. 123 defines the concept. In brief, the definition amounts to the following:

(1) A creditor who is owed at least £750 (unsecured) by the company has served a statutory notice on the company to pay or compound the debt and after three weeks has received no satisfaction from the company. (The rules here are the same as those with regard to the insolvent debtor in a private capacity, see Chapter 2.)

(2) An execution order or other court order for payment in favour of a creditor is returned unsatisfied in whole or in part.

(3) It is proved to the satisfaction of the court that the company is unable to pay its debts as they fall due.

(4) It is proved to the satisfaction of the court that the value of the company's assets is less than the amount of its liabilities, taking into account its contingent and prospective liabilities.

It should be noted that it is not necessary for a creditor to be owed in excess of £750 by the insolvent company in cases other than that in (1) above. (In practice an application will be rejected if the debt is less than £750.)

A useful example of point (4) is provided by the decision in *Taylors Industrial Flooring Ltd* v *M & H Plant Hire (Manchester) Ltd* (1990). M & H supplied plant to Taylors and invoiced that company in January 1989 and again the following month. Payment had not been received by April that year whereupon Taylors petitioned for the compulsory winding up of M & H. The Court of Appeal held that the petition was quite justified under s. 123 and could be heard in the usual way. This course of action by a dissatisfied creditor can often be more prudent than going through the formal demand process with the three week wait by which time the debtor company may well have gone under financially, leaving the creditor in a desperate situation.

In the Taylor case the debt was in fact undisputed. Thus the court was satisfied that the application was not being made purely to bring pressure on the debtor to pay a particular debt.

The procedure to be adopted in the compulsory liquidation

The petition

The petition may only be initiated by one or more jointly of the following under s. 124 of the Act:

(1) The company itself following a special resolution to that effect by shareholders.

(2) The directors following a board resolution agreeing to so act.

(3) A creditor or contributory.

(4) The Secretary of State (DTI) following a fraud investigation.

(5) The official receiver following an unsatisfactory voluntary liquidation.

(6) The Bank of England (concerning banks) and the Attorney General (concerning charities).

The petition must be served on the company at the registered office (unless the company is itself the petitioner), if possible in person. In addition, the petition must be advertised in the *London Gazette* not less than seven business days after service nor less than seven days before the hearing. It should be verified by affidavit, which is prima facie evidence of the statements in the petition. The Insolvency Rules, which control this aspect of the liquidation, also demand that copies of the petition are served on the administrator, AR, liquidator (if the company is already in voluntary liquidation) and the supervisor of any voluntary arrangement where such officials are in place in respect of the company. Other persons entitled to a copy of the document upon request with copying fee are directors, contributories or creditors.

Clearly the service of a petition on a debtor company is a drastic step for any creditor to take. Doubtless the creditor's primary wish is to recover his debt rather than to put the company out of business. The possibility of obtaining judgment against the company followed by (if necessary) enforcement by way of execution, garnishee or charging order proceedings may be considered. Then again, since the petition is not advertised in the *Gazette* until at least seven days after service on the company, the act of petitioning may itself produce the required funds. This tactic appears to be in line with current rules. Even so, wasting court time can be a serious matter.

Doubtless the directors will take a very serious view of a petition being made against the company. Discussions between directors and their advisers, e.g. solicitors, accountants and bankers, may well be advisable and remedial action may be taken to alleviate the position of the creditors.

Between the petition and the hearing

The crucial period between the petition and the hearing needs careful action by the directors. If a winding up order is made against the company at the hearing then the liquidation is deemed to have commenced at the date of the petition (s. 129 (2)). In addition, s. 127 of the Act specifies:

> In a winding up by the court any disposition of the company's property, and any transfer of shares, or alteration in the status of the company's members, made after the commencement of the winding up is, unless the court otherwise orders, void.

Thus, trading during this period may be extremely difficult if not impossible. The company's bank account will be frozen immediately the bank learns of the petition (usually through the *London Gazette*). *In Re Gray's Inn Construction Co Ltd* (1980) covers this ground. If trading is to be continued during this period an application to court under s. 127 for directions may be advisable (see Chapter 17 for further details of this part of the liquidation process).

The provisional liquidator

If it appears that on the lodging of a petition for winding up the assets of the company are in some jeopardy or the affairs of the business are not being conducted in a proper manner then the petitioner, the company, a creditor or the DTI may apply to the court for the appointment of a provisional liquidator. The application must be accompanied by an affidavit giving the grounds on which the appointment is required. If the court agrees and appoints such an officer (usually the official receiver), the powers given by the court to that person are specified and copies of the appointment are sent to the official receiver, if he is not to be the provisional liquidator, and also to any AR in office. Additionally, the provisional liquidator may apply to court for the appointment of a special manager, who need not be an IP, in cases where the nature of the company's business or the interests of the creditors indicate the necessity for this assistance (the Act s. 177). In brief, the role of the special manager is:

- to control and run the business;
- to preserve rather than realise assets;
- to be answerable to the provisional liquidator.

There is thus a considerable degree of damage limitation control in place where it is needed between the time of the petition and the order (if made). Often the fortunes of a company or the actions of the directors demand that strict action is taken immediately on behalf of the creditors to ensure that as much as possible is salvaged from the wreck.

The winding up order

Under the terms of the Act ss. 129 and 130, the winding up commences at the date of the petition (unless an earlier resolution has been passed for a voluntary winding up, in which case the date of the resolution applies). A copy of the order is sent to the Registrar of Companies for advertisement. By virtue of s. 136 (2) of the Act the official receiver becomes the liquidator and he continues until another person is appointed, if such becomes the case.

Where the liquidation follows a voluntary arrangement or an administration the court may appoint the supervisor of the arrangement or the administrator to be liquidator (s. 140).

The official receiver may by virtue of s. 137 of the Act apply to the Secretary of State for another person to be liquidator. Where the creditors fail to appoint a liquidator at the first meeting of creditors and the official receiver does not wish to act, the official receiver must refer the matter to the Secretary of State.

The statement of affairs

One of the first duties of the official receiver is to request information from present or past officers of the company and present or past (up to one year past) employees as appropriate in order that the statement of affairs may be compiled. They must provide the required facts within 21 days of this request unless special dispensation is given for a longer time period. Deponents must swear the statement by affidavit.

The statement may include accounts going back for three years (or more if the court so agrees).

By s. 131 of the Act the statement must include:

(a) particulars of the company's assets, debts and liabilities;

(b) names and addresses of creditors;

(c) securities held by creditors;

(d) dates when securities were respectively given;

(e) such further information as the official receiver may require.

The completed statement of affairs is sent to the court for filing.

Meeting of creditors

The Act s. 136 (4) and (5) specifies that the official receiver will decide within 12 weeks from the winding up order to hold a meeting of creditors. If, for any reason, he concludes that such a meeting is not necessary he must inform the court and the creditors of his reasons and in any case one quarter in value of the creditors can demand that such a meeting is held.

The creditors will be given 21 days' notice of the meeting and will receive proxy forms for completion if they do not intend to be at the meeting. In addition, proof of debt forms will also be enclosed with the agenda if they have not already been supplied to all known creditors.

The agenda for the first meeting of creditors is listed in the Insolvency Rules number 4.52 and will include the following matters:

(1) The appointment of a liquidator (or liquidators).

(2) A resolution to establish a liquidation committee.

(3) A resolution to define the liquidator's remuneration (if no resolution to establish a liquidation committee).

(4) A resolution to adjourn the meeting for not more than three weeks (if appropriate).

(5) Any other business the chairman may feel is fit for the meeting.

The quorum of this meeting shall be one person present in person or by proxy and voting shall be by majority in value of those present in person or by proxy, the value being the value of a valid claim lodged by proof form.

The official receiver or liquidator may call subsequent meetings of creditors to ascertain their general wishes and to inform them of progress in the winding up. Twenty-one days' notice of such meetings will be given.

The liquidation committee

The Act s. 141 covers the rules concerning the establishment of a liquidation committee. Such a committee is drawn from willing creditors and is usually formed at the first meeting of creditors. The liquidator may however call a meeting of creditors for the purpose of forming such a committee at any time and must do so if requested by a minimum of one-tenth in value of the creditors.

There is one exception to the above and that is on the occasion where the official receiver is the liquidator. No committee is then formed since its functions are carried out by the Secretary of State.

It is not always simple to find sufficient creditors willing to serve on this committee, which must consist of between three and five persons. Once the committee is formed, the chairman gives the liquidator a list of names and addresses of creditors who are willing to serve on it. The liquidator will issue his certificate of constitution as to the committee's existence and the certificate is then filed at court.

Whilst it may be seen that the role of the liquidation committee is largely supervisory and in fact the powers of such a group are limited it may well be that the existence of such a body is of considerable assistance to the liquidator. The knowledge and experience of the key creditors may afford the liquidator much specialised knowledge of the business in general and the company in question in particular. Clearly the liquidator will be guided in his decisions by this representative body of creditors. Certain actions of the liquidator in any case must have the sanction of the liquidation committee, e.g. payment of debts, compromise of claims, institution and defence of proceedings and the carrying on of business of the company, unless such actions have the sanction of the court (s. 167 (1) (a) and Schedule 4).

The liquidator's appointment

The liquidator may be appointed by the creditors or failing that by the court where, for instance, the creditors cannot agree on a suitable appointment or the liquidation follows an administration or CVA where the administrator or supervisor will step in as liquidator.

The liquidator must be an IP and have sufficient bonding (see Chapter 5).

The liquidator has enormous powers and duties in the winding up process as is evident from the minutiae of rules covering all aspects of the winding up. The effects of the liquidator's appointment are immediately apparent to all concerned with the winding up in whatever capacity. For example, from the date of the liquidator's appointment:

- contracts of employment – including those of directors – with the company are terminated;
- any disposition of the company's property is void without the court's sanction;
- any execution or distress or action against the company's property is void unless the court grants leave;
- the business of the company stops unless the court or liquidation committee gives approval.

The official receiver

It may be that, as already explained, the official receiver is liquidator at the time of the winding up order. However, whether or not the official receiver becomes the liquidator he continues to have close involvement with the proceedings. These duties are largely investigative in nature. Under the provisions of the Act ss. 131, 132 and 133 (investigation procedures) the official receiver will – as already mentioned – manage the production of the company's statement of affairs and will:

- if the company has failed, investigate the causes of failure;
- investigate the promotion, formation, business, dealings and affairs of the company;
- make such report to the court as he sees fit.

Clearly the conduct of the directors and any offences committed by them will come under scrutiny. Any misdemeanours by directors may then be subject to a report to the DTI for consideration within the terms of the Company Directors Disqualification Act 1986. The official receiver's report to court will either recommend no further action or that the papers be sent to the Crown Prosecution Service for further action.

According to rules numbers 4.43–4.46 of the Insolvency Rules (information to creditors) the official receiver shall send to all creditors at least once after the winding up order a full report covering the company's affairs and the progress of the winding up. He shall in addition file the report in court. He will also send to all creditors a summary of the company's statement of affairs together with any comments he sees fit to append.

Completion of the liquidation

Provided that the liquidator is not the official receiver he may summon a meeting of creditors for the purposes of:

● receiving the liquidator's report of the winding up;

● determining whether the liquidator may obtain his release (s. 146).

This meeting is subject to 28 days' notice to creditors and it will be advertised in the *London Gazette* at least one month before it is held. The liquidator will:

● account for his administration including the production of his receipts and payments;

● provide a statement that he has reconciled his account with that held by the Secretary of State in respect of the winding up.

Following the final meeting of creditors the liquidator will give notice to the court that the meeting has been held (sending a copy to the official receiver) and file notice of the meeting with the Registrar of Companies.

Where the official receiver is acting as liquidator he simply has to give notice to the Registrar of Companies that the winding up is complete and he is not bound to hold a meeting of creditors (s. 205 (1) (b)).

The Registrar of Companies shall register notice of the final meeting of creditors and, subject to objection from the Secretary of State on application from the official receiver or any other interested person, will erase the company name from the registry files on dissolution of the company at the end of the three month period from the date of receipt by him of such notice.

CHAPTER FIFTEEN

Corporate winding up: The secured creditor

The creditor's position

A crucial consideration in the liquidation process is the position of the creditor. The question is usually: 'How much shall I get – and when?' The answer is by no means straightforward and is subject to the rules laid down in the Insolvency Act 1986 and the Insolvency Rules 1986. Much depends on whether the creditor has any security interests (which can be many and varied) on the assets of the insolvent company. The rights of the creditor in a winding up situation are considerable and the liquidator often has a complicated set of issues to address. It may be helpful to examine the overall position of 'the creditor' by aligning the legal rules alongside the scenario often met in practice and then to consider the various options open to the creditor.

The order of distribution of monies by the liquidator

In a creditors' voluntary liquidation or a compulsory liquidation the order of payout of monies raised from the realisation of the insolvent company's assets is as follows.

Secured debts

Repayment from the value of any security takes place in so far as the assets secured are sufficient. (On occasion one sees the statement that such debts come first – it is safer to regard the secured debt as being apart from the unsecured one.)

Unsecured debts

The order of distribution of unsecured debts is:

- liquidator's fees and costs;
- preferential debts;
- debts secured by a floating charge (the word 'secured' is applied loosely here);
- unsecured debts, e.g. trade debts;
- deferred debts;
- shareholders – return of capital.

The secured creditor

The debenture holder

Definition

The debenture, which contains, say, a fixed charge over the company's fixed assets and a floating charge on the remainder of the assets, is commonplace. In addition the public issue of debentures which are quoted on a stock exchange may follow a similar pattern with the rights of the debenture holders being handled by a panel of trustees. The composition of charges in a debenture in favour of, say, the company's bankers, which is probably the most common type of debenture, may take a variety of forms. Thus, following the decisions in *Siebe Gorman & Co Ltd* v *Barclays Bank Ltd* (1979) and *Re Brightliffe Ltd* (1987) banks may now take a form of debenture which encompass a fixed charge on not only the company's fixed assets but also on some of the current assets. This device – if successful – may enhance the bank's position before the crystallisation of the floating charge although not necessarily after the event. Then again, the debenture may be wholly of the floating variety. The essentials of the floating charge will be covered in more detail later in this chapter.

The options open to the bank secured by the so called all monies debenture (the fixed and floating variety) by way of appointment of an AR have already been covered (see Chapter 12). Similarly the banker secured by such a debenture may realise some or all of the fixed assets piecemeal (aside from liquidation proceedings), before or after the commencement of liquidation.

The practical approach

It may be helpful now to refer to the specimen balance sheet extract on page 165 in order that a practical viewpoint can be established. In the example, one problem for the debenture holder may lie in the fact that whereas the Alpha factory is covered by the fixed charge (and properly scheduled in the charging clause in the debenture deed) the Beta property was purchased by XXX Manufacturing Co plc subsequent to the date of the debenture. In this situation it may transpire that the bank released a previous property from the fixed charge and the proceeds of sale of such property went to meet the costs of the new one – the Beta property. It is likely that the bank will have taken a supplemental deed by way of mortgage over the Beta property to bring it within the fixed charge element of the debenture.

If the company had purchased the Beta property with the assistance of another finance house then reference to the debenture deed will probably show that the bank's permission for such action must have been obtained. This being so, the bank will then only have a second charge by way of equitable mortgage over the new property, which interest will rank under the floating element of the debenture. If the company purchased the second property from its own funds without informing the bank then again the property will be attached to the debenture as an equitable interest only under the floating element of the debenture deed. Clearly the priorities when winding up a company will be affected. A crucial point with the fixed (legal) charge lies in the very nature of the charge. The legal charge enables the mortgagee to realise such security within the rules laid down in the Property Acts (e.g. Law of Property Act 1925) with comparative ease from the legal point of view (assuming there are no problems with an administrator or receiver). As will be seen the value of a floating (equitable) charge is much diminished from the secured lender's viewpoint.

The floating charge

The floating charge is a security interest over existing and future assets so that the debtor may continue to deal with them. The interest is equitable in nature. It cannot be a legal interest since the creditor, the debenture holder, cannot have any actual or constructive hold over the assets covered by the charge.

The floating charge can apply to a single asset or a class of assets and can attach to land, goods and choses in action, etc. In *Re Yorkshire Woolcombers Association Ltd* (1903) the judge stated that a floating charge had the following characteristics:

(1) It is a charge on the company's assets present and future.

(2) If the class of assets on which the floating charge is attached covers those assets which are used by the company in its ordinary trading activities then such assets must change from time to time.

(3) If by the charge it is contemplated that, until some future step is taken by or on behalf of those interested in the charge, the company may carry on its business in the ordinary way so far as it concerns the particular class of assets covered by the charge.

The basic purpose of the floating charge, which is unknown in some European jurisdictions and in the USA (although it has recently been incorporated into Scottish law) is that the company giving the charge can nevertheless give a good title over such asset to a purchaser. At the same time when specified events occur, e.g. receivership, liquidation, etc, or are automatic under the terms of the debenture deed the charge 'crystallises', that is it becomes 'fixed' in the hands of the chargee. The charge will of course still be equitable in nature. It can thus be seen that the floating charge hovers over the assets caught by the interest until such time as events occur which activate the charge in the creditor's favour.

Priorities

Generally speaking the priority of creditors' interests on the liquidation of a company depends on notice of prior charges to the creditor, type of charge, registration and other statutory rules in so far as the position of secured creditors is concerned. However, one obvious drawback to the floating charge from the creditors' point of view is that on the winding up of the company the interests of the preferential creditors come before those of the floating chargee. This was one powerful point behind the *Brightliffe* decision. In the case of *Siebe Gorman & Co Ltd* v *Barclays Bank Ltd* (1979) it was established that a fixed charge could indeed be taken over a current asset, e.g. book debts, only in so far as the chargee, the bank, had complete control over the asset. In the case in question the bank did indeed

Balance sheet (extract, given for example, not in full format)
The XXX Manufacturing Co Plc

(Assets side)

Fixed assets

		£	£
Property:	Alpha factory............................	XXX	
	Beta property......................................	XXX	XXX
Machinery			XXX
Plant			XXX
Ship			XXX
			XXX

Current assets

	£	
Stock	XXX	
Work in progress	XXX	
Finished goods	XXX	
Debtors	XXX	
Bills receivable	XXX	
Bank	XXX	
Cash	XXX	XXX
		XXX

(Liabilities side)

	£	
Capital	XXX	
Reserves	XXX	
Profit and loss	XXX	XXX
Debenture		XXX

Current liabilities

	£	
Creditors	XXX	
Bills payable	XXX	
Bank	XXX	XXX
		XXX

have such control since it comprised the proceeds of bills which the bank collected for the company and retained for its customer in a secure account.

The hardening rule: Definition

A further legal difficulty for the floating chargee is the so called hardening rule contained in s. 245 of the Act which states:

> Subject as follows a floating charge on the company's undertaking or property created at a relevant time is invalid except to the extent of the aggregate of:
>
> (a) the value of so much of the consideration for the creation of the charge as consists of money paid, or goods or services supplied, to the company at the same time as, or after, the creation of the charge.
>
> (b) the value of so much of that consideration as consists of the discharge or reduction, at the same time as, or after, the creation of the charge, of any debt of the company, and
>
> (c) the amount of such interest (if any) as is payable on the amount falling within paragraph (a) or (b) in pursuance of any agreement under which the money was so paid, the goods or services were so supplied or the debt was so discharged or reduced.

Section 245 of the Act further states that these rules operate from twelve months behind the onset of insolvency (i.e. a petition for winding up or administration) or two years where the lender is a connected person with the company.

The hardening rule: Practice

The general philosophy behind the somewhat complicated hardening rule appears to be based on the point that a powerful creditor, e.g. a bank, should not be able to obtain a floating charge on the undertaking of the company when the bank is already suspicious that the company is about to go under. The bank's position then as a secured creditor might be seen to constitute an unfair advantage over the body of unsecured creditors. Even so, such security could – as with any other type of charge – be attacked by the liquidator as a preference or even undervalue (see the case *Re M C Bacon* (1990) where the bank concerned was cleared of such charge, although the lesson is there). It is vital to appreciate that the following key points apply to s. 245:

(1) The floating charge must be taken within one year of the onset of insolvency (two years where a connected person is concerned).

(2) The company must be insolvent when the charge is taken. This may be difficult to prove in court.

A further important rule which has an impact on the workings of s. 245 is the so called rule in *Clayton's* case (*Devaynes* v *Noble* (1816)). This rule states that where a running debt is concerned, e.g. a current account, the first credits in repay the first debits out where the account is overdrawn. Thus, in the case of XXX Manufacturing Co plc, the item 'debenture' may be a fixed loan or a loan reducing on a structured time basis. However, the item 'bank' under 'current liabilities' would indicate a bank overdraft which, under the terms of the bank's debenture, would also be secured under such fixed and floating charge as detailed in the respective charging clause in the debenture bond. If, say, the debenture had been taken some ten months before the winding up petition it could well be that credits paid into the account after the debenture was taken more than wipe out the debt on the account on the date when the security was charged to the bank. This would mean that the entire overdraft on petition date was covered by the floating charge and could not be challenged. On the other hand, if the overdraft had been, say, £20 000 on the date of the charge and some £10 000 had been paid in and out of the account up to the date of petition, then half the overdraft would be covered by the charge and the other half would constitute an unsecured debt to the bank. The important question is whether the current account has been sufficiently active since the charge was taken (assuming the company was insolvent at that date).

Disadvantages of the floating charge

Disadvantages which attach a floating charge in favour of a lender, e.g. a bank, can be considerable. The stocks, work in progress and finished goods may be subject to reservation of title clauses in the contracts between the company and its suppliers (see section on reservation of title claim below). Furthermore, the value of the charge in reality may be slight since the current assets of the company – especially stocks – may be run down in the light of the financial difficulties faced by the company prior to liquidation. Admittedly the bank can call for periodic statements from the company of stock positions, debtors, sales orders, etc. but this may not provide much positive comfort. In addition, the presence of some powerful preferential creditors, e.g. Customs & Excise, may depreciate the value of the floating charge considerably when the full situation of the insolvent company comes to light. The floating charge may be a mixed blessing to the secured lender.

Quasi-security: The lien

Often a creditor may have a lien over company property in his possession. A lien may be defined as a right to retain possession of property belonging to a debtor until such time as the amount due has been paid. This 'quasi-security' is in effect a form of non-consensual security in the hands of the creditor (arising by operation of law) and it may provide the creditor with a valuable means of obtaining repayment of part or all of his debt. The right to exercise a lien is often open to a supplier of goods and services in circumstances where the supplier comes into possession of documents or papers belonging to the company customer or others claiming through the company. For instance, businesses such as carriers by road, sea or air, freight forwarders, sellers of goods, port authorities, warehouses, distributors, hotel keepers, garage owners, banks, accountants and other professional persons may all have occasion to exercise a lien.

The make-up of a lien

Essential elements of a lien are:

- possession of the goods or documents of title to those goods;
- a debt presently due and payable by the customer (owner of the goods in question).

Normally the lien does not arise until the debt behind the lien is payable. In addition, the goods or documents of title must be obtained by the creditor in the normal course of business, i.e. not received by stealth or fraud. A lien is not a charge as such on the goods and thus no registration is necessary. (It may just be that a lien clause in, say, a contract of sale may require registration under the terms of the Companies Act 1985 s. 395, although that may be doubtful in so far as the lien arises by operation of law and is not created by the company.) A lien cannot be a claim to title of the goods in question.

How a lien may arise

The lien can arise in one of three ways:

(1) *As a common law right* The long established 'carrier's lien' is one example. Also, the case *Brandao* v *Barnett* (1846) established the special rights of lien available to a lending bank in so far as the bank's lien also carries the right to sell, i.e. the proceeds of items of value belonging to a borrowing customer can be applied to repayment of that customer's debt with the bank.

(2) *By express agreement* The seller can incorporate in the standard terms and conditions of the contract of sale a lien clause. The bank often takes a specific letter of lien covering items owned by a customer in the hands of the bank in the course of day to day business (this is not safe custody, which is a specific contract of bailment). This type of lien is known as a 'contractual lien' since it arises by specific agreement.

(3) *By statute* This might be a lien created in favour of an unpaid seller of goods by virtue of s. 39 of the Sale of Goods Act 1979.

It is vital to the maintenance of the lien that the seller retains possession of the goods or documents of title to those goods, e.g. a warehouse-keeper's receipt. However, if documents or goods are released by the seller to the buyer but then come into the seller's hands again at a later date (in a lawful manner), the seller's lien may be good. Points of detail are important here, e.g. goods stored in a buyer's warehouse in circumstances where a lender, e.g. the company's bank, holds the documents of title to such goods may cause problems for the bank. The goods should be held in an independent warehouse and the requisite receipt for such goods should be made out in the bank's name.

Types of lien

There are basically two specific types of lien, each carrying different rights. They are:

(1) *The specific or particular lien* This lien gives a right only over the actual goods which are the subject of the unpaid debt. Such a right of lien does not extend to any other goods of the debtor which may be in the temporary possession of the creditor.

(2) *The general lien* This type of lien is a right to retain all the owner's goods in possession pending payment of a debt whether or not those goods are related to the debt itself. Unless a general lien clause is inserted into the contract of sale, the possibility of the seller having a general lien on his customer's goods is rare at common law. Basically only certain persons, e.g. solicitors and bankers have a general lien on customer's goods and papers as of right.

The seller's rights

The rights of the unpaid seller who has a possessory lien over the goods of the buyer initially give the seller the right to retain the goods pending payment. However, in practical terms the seller will seek to sell the goods elsewhere and recoup his debt. Normally the right to sell is expressly included in a lien clause and, provided the seller follows the terms of that clause to the letter, e.g. giving notice to the buyer of pending sale, the problem is solved. Occasionally the seller has statutory rights of sale. Alternatively, application may be made to court by an unpaid seller for permission to sell goods held by him under lien. In summary, four ways are open to the seller to exercise a right of sale as follows:

(1) By the inclusion of a suitable clause in the sale contract.

(2) By statute, e.g. Sale of Goods Act 1979. Here, before the seller can proceed to sell the goods under lien the date for payment by the buyer must have passed or the purchaser must be insolvent and known to be unable to pay.

(3) By giving three months' notice to the buyer under the Torts (Interference with Goods) Act 1977 that sale of the goods will commence unless payment is received in the meantime and the purchaser collects the goods where they are still in the seller's hands.

(4) By application to court for sale to take place where provisions (1)–(3) above do not apply.

The insolvency situation

When insolvency proceedings have commenced against the debtor in circumstances where an unpaid creditor claims a lien over the debtor's goods, then the creditor shall be regarded as a secured creditor to the extent of the value of the goods in question.

It should be mentioned that a lien over any books, papers or other records of a company in insolvency is unenforceable to the extent that enforcement of such lien would deprive an administrator, liquidator or provisional liquidator of those records when an 'office holder' is in need of them. (s. 246 of the Act). Moreover, s. 11 (3) of the Act also provides that when an administration order has been made against a company no lien may be enforced by a creditor except with the consent of the administrator or the leave of court.

It is thus evident that the force of a valid lien claim in the hands of a creditor may prove to be a valuable asset. It is strange that there are relatively few recorded case decisions from the courts in this area of insolvency.

Quasi-security: The reservation of title claim

A further form of quasi-security may be effected through the insertion of a 'reservation of title' (ROT) clause in a sale contract by the seller whereby the buyer is denied legal ownership of the goods until payment has been made in full. In this way the liquidator of the XXX Manufacturing Co plc (see page 165) – or indeed the holder of a floating charge on the assets of that company – may well be denied a substantial portion of the value of such assets in the liquidation of the business. The ROT claim could affect the realisation of the stocks, work in progress, finished goods, possibly the debtor's figure and even the bank balance.

Definition

The basic premise of the ROT clause in a sale contract covering goods is simple enough. A distinction is drawn between legal ownership and possession. A straightforward ROT clause might read as follows:

> Unless the company shall otherwise specify in writing all goods sold by the company to the purchaser shall be and remain the property of the company [i.e. the seller] until the full purchase price thereof shall be paid to the company.

The simple ROT clause seeks to address the problems which can arise for the unpaid seller of goods when a company faces liquidation. The Sale of Goods Act 1979 specifies that title in goods passes on or before delivery unless the parties agree otherwise. Once title to goods has passed then the only recourse open to the seller is to sue – or prove his debt in the winding up of – the company. The realisation of a debt in such circumstances often produces only a small percentage of the full amount. It is however open to the contracting parties to 'agree otherwise' than that normal circumstances will apply regarding the passing of title of the goods. In the absence of the ROT clause in a sale contract title to the goods may pass at contract stage, when the goods are ready for delivery, or even on delivery itself – it depends on the wording of the agreement. The ROT system simply delays the passing of the title in the goods to post delivery stage, i.e. when payment is made for the goods as such or even when all outstanding monies have been settled between seller and buyer.

The use of the ROT claim

There is nothing new in the ROT system of selling. Indeed, it has been possible for many years in the United Kingdom and has been used extensively over the years in the rest of Europe – particularly Germany and Holland. Whereas a cornucopia of court decisions has become available in recent years, the decades before the 1970s were almost devoid of precedents. In 1976 the celebrated case *Aluminium Industrie Vaassen BV* (a Dutch exporter of aluminium sheet panels) v *Romalpa Aluminium Ltd* (a UK importer) paved the way for complicated developments in this arm of the law. The Dutch company had sold sheet panels to the UK company under contracts containing simple ROT clauses. When the UK company went into liquidation the liquidator faced a claim from the Dutch exporter for the return of aluminium sufficient to clear outstanding debts between the two companies. The Dutch company was successful in its claim to the detriment of the liquidator. It transpired that the Dutch company was able to identify the respective sheets of aluminium in the storage area on the Romalpa premises and equate such items with the relative unpaid invoices. However, events in later court cases have proved that the ROT claim has become increasingly fraught with difficulties. The more sophisticated the ROT clause becomes, the more complicated are the underlying circumstances.

ROT problem areas

An IP and an unpaid seller faced with an ROT situation in a claim for debt repayment or in a liquidation must face up to three fundamental aspects of the ROT clause:

(1) Can the goods in question be accurately identified?

(2) Has the contract for sale, and especially the ROT clause, been properly drafted and agreed by the contracting parties?

(3) Does the ROT clause in the sale contract stand up in law as a properly enforceable right of the seller?

Identification

This may be the most difficult part of the claim for the seller to uphold. It will be necessary for the seller to match goods on site at the buyer's premises with unpaid invoices. Have the goods in question been marked or separately stored? The goods may be stacked up with similar goods from another source. The goods under review may have been sold on. This is perfectly in order since the Sale of Goods Act 1979 s. 25 allows for this provided it was not forbidden in the original sale contract. A more difficult problem for the seller is when 'admixture' has taken place with the goods. This indicates that the buyer has changed the goods in the manufacturing process or else has enhanced the goods in some way to render them fit for onsale. The buyer may well have bought raw materials which were then processed in such a way as to render the original purchased goods totally unidentifiable.

Listed below are several interesting cases concerning admixture of raw materials which have been reported in recent years.

Re Bond Worth Ltd (1979)
Fibres had been purchased for processing into carpets. The fibres had been dyed during the manufacturing process. The seller – Monsanto – was unable to extract the fibres free of dye. In order that the seller could claim title to the finished product, i.e. the carpets, a charge would have been necessary and none was so registered. The claim failed.

Clough Mill Ltd v Martin (1984)
The circumstances were similar to those in the *Bond Worth* case and the claim similarly failed.

Borden (UK) Ltd v Scottish Timber Products Ltd (1979)
The contract for sale involved glue to be used in the manufacture of chipboard. Clearly the admixture process was total and there could be no question of recovery of the raw material, i.e. the glue.

Hendy Lennox (Industrial Engines) Ltd v Graham Puttick Ltd (1984)
The *Hendy Lennox* case did in fact bring a small measure of relief to the unpaid seller who had sold diesel engines which had been bolted on to generator equipment. In so far as the engines had not been changed from their original state and it was possible to have them removed from the generators, the ROT claim could hold good and the goods be recovered by the seller. Unfortunately for the seller, however, it transpired that many of the generators in question had

been sold on to third parties and thus could not be recovered. This case highlights the complexities of the ROT claim and the importance of the practical circumstances surrounding each case.

Re Peachdart Ltd (1984)

The *Peachdart* case also demonstrates the difficulties surrounding the ROT claim. Here the argument concerned the sale of leather to a buyer, who used such goods in the manufacture of handbags. The leather obviously existed as such and could be seen and handled. However, the leather as sold bore little resemblance to the leather as seen in the finished goods. Identification was clearly impossible. The ROT clause attempted to attach work in progress and finished goods arising from the leather and even covered proceeds from the sale of the handbags. The court was not impressed with this 'all bells and whistles' clause because it was seen as a possible charge over sales and as such was void for want of registration under the terms of s. 395 of the Companies Act 1985.

The *Peachdart* case is particularly interesting in that the concept of the creation of a 'trust' status between seller and buyer was considered. A clause in the underlying contract read:

> Until the seller is paid in full for all the products the relationship of the buyer to the seller shall be fiduciary in respect of the products or other goods in which they are incorporated or used and if the same are sold by the buyer the seller shall have the right to trace the proceeds thereof according to the principles in *Re Halletts Estate* (1880). A like right for the seller shall apply where the buyer uses the products in any way so as to be entitled to payment from a third party.

Several points arise here. Firstly, the word 'fiduciary' (line two of the clause) is illuminating. Presumably the intention of the seller is to have a trust relationship with the buyer so that the buyer holds the original goods, finished product, or even sale proceeds on trust for the seller pending payment of the invoice in full – such arrangement to be good against a liquidator. A clause such as that above is invariably thrown out by the court for a number of reasons. The 'charge' argument (see the *Peachdart* case above) may be raised. The finished product may contain raw materials from two sellers with consequent problems of apportionment of value.

Secondly, the case *Re Halletts Estate* (1880) attempts to cater for the position where sale proceeds are traced to the buyer's bank account and as such are lost through the operation of *Clayton's* rule in so far as trust funds come outside *Clayton's* case.

It is thus apparent that the practical considerations relevant to the use of an ROT clause in a sale contract are of paramount importance. The simple truth is that the courts will not allow such clauses to operate effectively where there is any suspicion that the seller is attempting to gain unfair advantage over the buyer company's other creditors. Various legal problems impact on the whole matter, e.g. the question of the clause being a registrable charge or a trust instrument.

The effectiveness of the ROT clause from a practical point of view seems to hinge on whether the original goods sold to the buyer have been subject to admixture and whether the goods are on site at the buyer's premises or whether they have been sold on to ultimate buyers either in the raw state or as part of a manufactured product.

Has the contract of sale been properly drafted (particularly the ROT clause) and agreed by the contacting parties?

It may be argued that there are several forms of agreement, e.g. the quotation, the order form, confirmation of order or delivery note apart from the underlying sale contract where the ROT should be quoted. This assumes that there was in fact a specific contract of sale in written form in the first place. Then again, the seller may attempt to change the conditions of the ROT clause during the course of dealing with a buyer. It would seem that the delivery note is probably the crucial document in the chain of events and the seller would do well to ensure that the buyer has his attention drawn to the ROT clause in such document and can prove that the buyer has agreed to such terms. Verbal evidence on its own is of little use although a proven agreed history of trading under such previously agreed dealings would be useful.

Does the ROT clause in the sale contract (of whatever nature) stand up in law as a properly enforceable right of the seller?

The legal problems surrounding the wording of the ROT clause have already been covered. The various cases mentioned (there are many others) evidence the minefield awaiting the seller attempting to tie a buyer down in an ROT situation. Thus, questions of admixture, possible trust application and onsale of goods to third parties may all be present. All that can be suggested here is that the initial negotiations between buyer and seller cover all foreseen circum-stances surrounding the storage of the goods, timing of the processing of the goods, sales of the goods and ultimate payment by the buyer. The seller would then be advised to have any ROT clauses clearly shown in the relevant documentation and patently agreed to by the buyer. It may be argued at this point that the whole business of sales under reservation of title agreements is not only extremely complex but often results in considerable doubt on the part of the seller as to its general efficacy in commercial terms.

Conclusions

It is apparent that the growth of the secured claim by the creditor who is secured by either legal or equitable mortgage, charge or assignment (as appropriate) over one or more assets of the corporate debtor, is complex. Moreover, the creditor may be secured expressly or by implication or even have a claim against the company by way of quasi-security. The options open to the secured creditor – and, more importantly the partly secured creditor (where the value of the security is less than the debt it secures) – are similar to those open to the secured creditor of an insolvent individual's estate. The rules in those circumstances are covered in Chapter 6. It is up to the secured creditor to decide whether or not he needs to prove his debt and, if he does, to agree the value of his security with the liquidator. If he fails to follow this course he may not be able to receive a dividend covering any shortfall in security value or vote at a creditors' meeting.

CHAPTER SIXTEEN

Corporate winding up: The unsecured creditor

Once an insolvency becomes known the unsecured creditors will start to wonder how much they are likely to recover of what is owed to them and when they are likely to recover part or all of their debt. Obviously one cannot be specific on these points but it can be said that in cases where the directors of the insolvent company have seen the danger signs early on and have taken remedial steps to lessen the effect on the creditors, the ultimate losses may not be too great. Be that as it may, the liquidator will follow the many rules contained in the Act (and the Rules) when the time arrives for him to commence repayment of the company's debts – in so far as he is able to do so.

Preferential debts

Once the liquidator's fees and expenses are recovered from the realisation of company assets, the preferential creditors may expect some return on their debts. The schedule of preferential debts is contained in Schedule 6 of the Act and this matter has already been covered as far as the individual debtor is concerned in Chapter 8. Sections 386 and 387 of the Act refer to relevant dates where the preferential debt is concerned. Briefly, the preferential debt in so far as a company is concerned is that which exists on the date of the making of an administration order, the date of approval of a CVA, the date of the passing of a resolution for winding up, the date of the appointment of a provisional liquidator or the date of the winding up order, whichever date is appropriate. All preferential debts are treated equally by the liquidator. The *pari passu* treatment of all creditors is strictly applied and no one creditor receives more favourable treatment than the others.

The list of preferential creditors contained in Schedule 6 of the Act as referred to in ss. 386 and 387 of the Act (preferential debts in company and individual insolvency) was, as has been stated, covered in Chapter 8. However, the question of the preferential aspect of monies owed to employees needs further examination. Where a third party advances money to an insolvent company for payment of wages, the lender subrogates the rights of the employees in so far as repayment of those monies is still outstanding within the limits of the rules contained in Schedule 6 of the Act. The practical application of these rules, so far as the bank is concerned, depends on exactly how the bank has recorded the transactions during the relevant time period.

The wages account

In the absence of any special arrangements before the winding up petition in respect of the payment of wages, cheques which have been debited to the company's account, covering monies borrowed to pay wages, may be classified as forming a preferential claim in the bank's hands. The overdraft at the bank in the company's name on petition date will constitute wages in so far as such debits have not been repaid by further credits received subsequently for the account and thus wiped out by the operation of *Clayton's* rule. If the current account is fast moving it could be that only the most recent wages cheques are still outstanding. To alleviate the diminution in the bank's claim in this respect a special wages account may have been opened in the company's name by the bank on an earlier date, whereby all cheques cashed for wages were segregated and the overdraft on that account would rank for preferential status (within the limitations of the rules). Once the account had been running for more than 16 weeks the application of the wages cheque for week 17 would be matched by a transfer from the general account of the company (even if this adds to the existing debt on that account) to the wages account to repay the wages account debit for week one. It has to be said that this depends on whether the bank had concerns over the company's position and took the steps listed above within 16 weeks of the crash. It would assist the bank if all cheques cashed from the wages account were clearly drawn to wages and a certificate taken from the secretary of the company at regular intervals to the effect that all such monies drawn from the wages account were applied in payment of wages. Even so, the limit placed upon wages debts for preferential status is currently limited to wages paid to an employee for the previous four months behind the relevant date and shall not exceed £800 per employee. The agreement as to what the final figure is for preferential status must be a matter of negotiations between the bank and the liquidator once the employees' wages records are obtained.

Set-off

Frequently the chances of repayment for the creditor of a company which is in liquidation may depend on the rules of statutory set-off. Where a company has more than one account with the insolvent company and one account is in credit and another is in debit when liquidation commences then the rules of set-off will assist the creditor.

While set-off has already been covered in Chapter 8, it may nevertheless be useful to examine some practical aspects of this matter as it applies to the corporate body.

The question concerning corporate set-off is that of the mutuality of the balances involved. The word 'due' has already been mentioned. If a bank had given a large performance bond on behalf of a corporate customer and relied on a credit balance kept by that company with the bank as evidence of the customer's means it would be in a very difficult position if the liquidator could demand the credit balance and the bank was then called under its bond. If the bank happens to hold security, e.g. a debenture, from the company and all other liabilities of the company to the bank have been cleared apart from a bond – a contingent liability – the bank may nevertheless refuse to discharge the debenture until the bond is cancelled (*Re Rudd and Sons Ltd* (1986)). In any case, the bank will hold a counter-indemnity from the company to cover the contingent liability behind the bond although that counter-indemnity may not be worth much in a liquidation.

Statutory set-off is mandatory, i.e. the bank has no choice in the matter (subject to rules concerning trusts covered earlier, see page 88). The case of *National Westminster Bank Ltd* v *Halesowen Pressworks & Assemblies Ltd* (1972) made this clear (even so this case decision was grounded on s. 31 of the Bankruptcy Act 1914, the forerunner of the Insolvency Act 1986). As to the crucial matter of the availability of credit funds for set-off against a contingent debt, it is suggested that the solution is not exactly settled although it is thought that the word 'due' quoted above from the Act and Rules must mean 'due at the time the contract is entered into under which a debt may become due, regardless of when it actually becomes due'. With this measure of optimism the bank (and indeed any other creditor in a similar situation) may prove for the net debt on the accounts under scrutiny with confidence.

A further situation may arise covering the rights of the creditor to set off credit and debit balances in its books on the insolvency of a debtor customer. It may happen – particularly in the context of a company's relationship with its bank – that the bank holds three accounts in the name of a corporate customer as follows:

No 1 account: credit   £40 000

No 2 account: overdraft £60 000

No 3 account: overdraft £30 000

Suppose that the overdraft for £60 000 on the No 2 account is preferential, i.e. it represents wages payments. The bank's best position would be to set off the credit balance against the No 3 account overdraft thus wiping it out and applying the resulting £10 000 credit to the No 2 account. The bank thus would prove for £50 000 as a preferential creditor. The liquidator would hardly be agreeable to this. Alternatively, it would be unfair to expect the bank to apply the full credit balance towards the No 2 account. Fortunately the decision in *Re Unit 2 Windows Ltd* (1985) provides an equitable solution (see also page 91). This case gives a ruling that the bank has to apply the credit balance rateably between the preferential and non-preferential debts so that twice the credit monies are applied to the No 2 account than to the No 3 account. The available credit balance is utilised rateably to the two classes of debt. Thus the bank would prove as a preferential creditor for £33 334 and as an ordinary creditor for £16 666.

Ordinary debts

Next in line after the preferential creditors (where the unsecured creditor is concerned) is the main body of creditors. These are known as ordinary creditors. Rules covering claims and proof, etc. have been covered in Chapter 6.

Non-provable debts

Debts not capable of being proved – and therefore of being recovered – in a liquidation (except as covered below) include:

- debts incapable of being fairly estimated;
- illegal debts;
- foreign tax claims;
- statute barred debts (out of time debts – a typical time period being six years).

The exceptions to the 'irrecoverable nature' of the debts (even though not provable) are fines and maintenance order payments, which have to be paid in full by a bankrupt. In the context of the corporate winding up these will not be applicable.

CHAPTER SEVENTEEN

Corporate winding up: Further provisions

Whereas the Insolvency Act 1986 brought together all the existing provisions pertaining to the bankruptcy of the individual and the corporate winding up, the difference in the legal make-up of the two situations has of necessity brought some important differences within the rules pertaining to the insolvent bankruptcy and the corporate compulsory liquidation. Vital considerations regarding the position of the company director in a company winding up have recently emerged through current legislation and court decisions. In addition, an understanding of the VAT relief available to the creditor in a liquidation (or in a 'sole trader' situation) and the remuneration of the liquidator in a company insolvency (and the trustee in a bankruptcy) is needed. These topics are discussed in this final chapter in order to complete the picture of insolvency law and practice.

Dispositions

The duties of the liquidator will include *inter alia* a close examination of the books of the insolvent company and the latest bank statements, invoices, correspondence, etc. The authority of the company director to dispose of the assets (in whatever form) of an insolvent company normally ceases on the gazetting of the petition promulgating the forthcoming liquidation.

Commencement date of the liquidation

The commencement date of the liquidation in the case of a members' voluntary winding up is the date of the members' respective resolution to liquidate. When a company is being wound up by means of a compulsory liquidation the commencement date is the date of the petition unless there was a prior resolution to wind up voluntarily, in which case it remains the date of the resolution.

Void dispositions

Where a company disposes of assets subsequent to the commencement date such dispositions shall be void against the liquidator without the sanction of the court (s. 127 of the Act). Any payment into an overdrawn account of the company at the bank would thus be repayable and any debit to the account, which would have the effect of increasing an existing overdraft, would not even be provable (once the petition is advertised). The court will take into account the interests of all pre-liquidation creditors before exercising its discretion and making a validation order covering dispositions which would otherwise be void. It is very likely that such an order would be granted on condition that continued trading (if decided upon) would be at a profit and for the benefit of the creditors as a whole. It would be best for the bank to obtain the prior approval of the court to such transactions.

The decision in *Re Gray's Inn Construction Co Ltd* (1980) is interesting in that the Court of Appeal held that both payments into a bank account of £25 000 and payments out of the account amounting to £24 000 after the commencement date of winding up were dispositions within the meaning of s. 127 of the Act (the account being overdrawn). Since the bank would benefit by payments in and the company's creditors similarly would gain from the payments out it was seen as inequitable that those creditors should be paid in full for debts incurred by the company when other creditors may have to be satisfied with only a dividend in due course.

However, the general position regarding payments in and out of a bank account which is in credit has until recently been somewhat unclear. The *Barne Crown Ltd* (1994) case covered such a position and the discussion in court revolved around the point that the bank, in collecting a cheque for a company whose account was in credit, in fact was performing essentially an agency function as a collecting banker. The court analysed the collection process and the exact time when the disposition (if any) occurred and by whom it was made. The conclusion appeared to uphold the view that where a bank account of an insolvent company is in credit and money is paid into that account (thereby increasing the existing credit balance) no disposition takes place of the property of the customer in favour of the bank. There is in reality only an adjustment of the entries in the statement recording the accounts between the customer and the bank. This somewhat esoteric point could presumably assist a bank which has an account of an insolvent company in its books and finds that on liquidation of the company the full amount of the credit balance in the name of the company is available for set-off against a debit balance in the name of the company, which also appears in the books of the bank.

Voidable transactions

The rules concerning certain transactions which the trustee in bankruptcy may upset whilst trawling through the bankrupt's estate have already been covered in Chapter 7. Similar rules for such dealings apply equally to the liquidation or administration of a company and are encapsulated in ss. 238–246 under the heading 'Adjustment of prior transactions (administration and liquidation)'.

The following types of dealing apply.

Transactions at undervalue

Section 238 (4) of the Act states:

A company enters a transaction at undervalue with a person when:

(a) the company makes a gift to that person or otherwise enters into a transaction with that person on terms that provide for the company to receive no consideration, or

(b) the company enters into a transaction with that person for a consideration the value of which, in money or money's worth, is significantly less than the value, in money or money's worth of the consideration provided by the company.

However, s. 238 (5) goes on to state:

The court shall not make an order under this section in respect of a transaction at an undervalue if it is satisfied:

(a) that the company which entered into the transaction did so in good faith and for the purpose of carrying on its business, and

(b) that at the time it did so there were reasonable grounds for believing that the transaction would benefit the company.

As mentioned in Chapter 15, a bank was attacked by a liquidator for having accepted a security at an undervalue (*Re M C Bacon* (1990) where a bank had taken a floating charge over the assets of the borrowing company). The bank was cleared of the accusation since it appeared that the court held the view that such a charge (a floating charge on the company assets) was incapable of valuation as such. However, perhaps if a charge taken by a bank (or indeed any other creditor) over a borrowing company's assets clearly covers a stated amount (and is not a charge of the 'unlimited' variety) the court's attitude would be different.

The timing of this type of transaction is important. Section 240 states that the undervalue must be made during the two-year period ending with the presentation of a petition for an administration order or for winding up. Furthermore, it has to be proved that at the time the alleged undervalue was made the company was either already insolvent, i.e. unable to pay its debts, or became insolvent as a result of the undervalue.

Section 241 gives the court diverse powers to make whatever order is suitable for rectification of an undervalue such as the restoration of property comprised in the transaction to the company for the benefit of all the creditors. The recipient of the undervalue would then have to prove as a creditor with the others in whatever distribution is made in due course by the liquidator.

It would seem that the above provisions are wide in their application. Deals such as the selling of company goods to associate companies at cut prices or, say, the directors selling equipment, etc. to themselves at reduced rates (despite provisions in the Companies Act which may cover such practices) could be interpreted as undervalues.

It is likely that in practice the court will not make an order under s. 238 (quoted above) lightly since the manifest intention behind these rules is to avoid unfairness to creditors in general (especially at the expense of giving the directors of the insolvent company an unfair advantage). A possible scenario where an order could be granted would be where a company disposes of one of its properties (valued at £1 000 000) for a sum of £500 000. The directors made it clear in the board resolution covering the sale that the transaction was solely to give the company much needed funds to settle urgent suppliers' bills. The directors manifestly did not gain from the sale in any way – other than by preserving their jobs as directors. Prior to the respective board meeting, the directors had obtained advice from the company's auditors as to the efficacy of the sale and the urgency of avoiding imminent insolvency (or even rectifying possible existing insolvency). It would be important to prove that the board had acted 'in good faith' and the approval of the shareholders (if different from the directors) would be an additional help in meeting the court's requirements. The tests are somewhat subjective, but are clear although not easy to meet.

The preference

The concept of the preference as it applies to the company is similar to that in the bankruptcy of the individual (see Chapter 7). Section 239 states:

> Where the company has at a relevant time [six months prior to the petition for an administration order or liquidation and within two years prior to such petition where the preference is in favour of an associate] given a preference to any person, the office-holder [administrator or liquidator] may apply to court for an order under this section [transfer of such property/money forming the preference back to the company]...

Furthermore a company gives a preference to a person if:

> (a) that person is one of the company's creditors or a surety or guarantor for any of the company's debts or other liabilities, and
>
> (b) the company does anything or suffers anything to be done which (in either case) has the effect of putting that person into a position which, in the event of the company going into insolvent liquidation, will be better than the position he would have been in if that thing had not been done.

Again – as with the undervalue – the company must either be insolvent when the preference is made or become so as a result of the transaction.

Possible examples of the preference (as it applies to the company) may be:

(1) Diverting all available funds to repaying the company's bank overdraft with the intention of having a director's guarantee in favour of the company (and any supporting security) cancelled by the bank.

(2) A supplier which is an associated company.

(3) Repaying a director's loan to the company ahead of normal trade suppliers contrary to established practice with such suppliers. Thus, trade creditors suffer in order that a director's loan is cleared before the crash, leaving the creditors in a worse position that they should otherwise have been in.

Extortionate credit transactions

Once again the provisions covering extortionate credit transactions are similar to those applied in individual insolvency. Section 244 (3) states:

> For the purposes of this section a transaction is extortionate if, having regard to the risk accepted by the person providing the credit:
>
> (a) the terms of it are or were such as to require grossly exorbitant payments to be made (whether unconditionally or in certain contingencies) in respect of the provision of credit, or
>
> (b) it otherwise grossly contravened ordinary principles of fair dealing, and it shall be presumed, unless the contrary is proved, that a transaction with respect to which an application is made under this section is or, as the case may be, was extortionate.

Extortionate credit transactions under s. 244 must have been made within a period of three years ending on the day an administration order is made or the company went into liquidation. The court may make any appropriate order to rectify this type of transaction (including setting aside in whole or in part any obligation created by it).

VAT relief

The current system whereby unpaid sellers may obtain relief on the VAT element of their debts has been in operation since July 1990.

Purpose of VAT relief

The purpose of VAT relief is to enable a supplier to avoid having to pay output tax to H M Customs and Excise on sales made by him in circumstances when he has not been paid and the debt turns out to be bad. To come within the current VAT relief scheme the debts in question must be at least six months old from the date of supply (the sale) and such debts must have been written off in the supplier's books as being uncollectable.

Procedure

The procedure in connection with VAT relief is straightforward. The seller will have invoiced the buyer for the full amount of goods sold to him including VAT (where the seller is registered for VAT purposes in the normal way). The seller's position is that he has settled the VAT element of the sale with the Customs but is unable to collect the invoice value from the buyer. The seller will proceed as follows:

(1) The seller will prove in the (eventual) insolvency of the buyer for the full amount of the debt (including VAT). The VAT element may constitute in whole or in part a preferential claim in the seller's hands.

(2) The seller will then reclaim the VAT element in the sale direct from the Customs and Excise.

(3) If the seller receives repayment of the debt in the insolvency of the buyer in whole or (more likely) in part, he will have to repay the Customs and Excise that part of the dividend received from the trustee/liquidator which relates to VAT in the original claim.

Disqualification and personal liability for fraudulent and wrongful trading

A consideration of corporate insolvency law would not be complete without a study of the effects of both fraudulent and wrongful trading on the insolvent company and any director(s) concerned. Indeed, considerations covering the concepts of both fraudulent trading and wrongful trading also attach to the 'shadow director', who, in relation to a company, is a person in accordance with whose directions or instructions the directors of the company are accustomed to act (but so that a person is not deemed to be a shadow director by reason only that the directors act on advice given by him in a professional capacity; s. 251 of the Act).

Thus, to be a shadow director (and possibly attract the disqualification provisions of the Company Directors Disqualification Act 1986) the person concerned (not being a professional adviser, e.g. the company solicitor or accountant) must be proven to have made significant financial and/or commercial decisions as to how the company has been run and to have had the authority to have them carried out. Thus shareholders, associates of the directors or managers of the business (or even the company's bankers) may fall into this category.

Fraudulent trading

Fraud on the part of a director – as against mere negligence – is a very serious matter and it attracts criminal liability whether or not the company is in the course of being wound up. Thus, continuing to trade whilst the company is (or may be) insolvent, without knowing or caring whether creditors will be paid or not could constitute fraudulent trading. For civil liability and penalties in this matter one may refer to s. 4 of the Company Directors Disqualification Act 1986 which states:

> The court may make a disqualification order against a person if, in the course of the winding up of a company, it appears that he
>
> (a) has been guilty of an offence for which he is liable (whether he has been convicted or not) under section 458 of the Companies Act ... fraudulent trading ... or
>
> (b) has been otherwise guilty, while an officer or liquidator of the company or receiver or manager of its property, of any fraud in relation to the company or of any breach of his duty as such officer, liquidator, receiver or manager.

Whilst no minimum period for disqualification as a director (or manager by whatever name called) is laid down in this Act the maximum disqualification period the court can impose is 15 years under this section.

Furthermore, ss. 213 and 214 of the Insolvency Act 1986 cover civil liability of any directors guilty of fraudulent or wrongful trading by giving the court discretion to order that such persons shall make contributions from their private resources to the company's assets.

Wrongful trading

Whilst the concept of fraudulent trading has been encapsulated in company law for a considerable time, the concept of wrongful trading was introduced by the 1986 Act. Section 214 states that a person who is or has been a director (or a shadow director, i.e. a person not being a director – or indeed employed by the company as such at all – but whose advice and direction the company has consistently followed) may as a result of his conduct in managing (or mismanaging) the company also be required to contribute towards the assets of the company in liquidation. The requirements of s. 214 are as follows:

(1) The company has gone into insolvent liquidation.

(2) Before the commencement of the liquidation, the director concerned knew (or ought to have known) that there was no reasonable prospect that liquidation could be avoided.

(3) The person concerned was a director or shadow director at the time.

Thus in both ss. 213 and 214 the company in question shall be in liquidation and (apart from any question of criminal liability in the case of fraud by the director) the options of both disqualification and contribution are available to the court.

In the case of wrongful trading it may be seen that the rule is somewhat objective. This is thought to be deliberate and indeed beneficial to the business community. Thus, where a liquidator makes a s. 214 application, the court will not make an order against the director if it is satisfied that he took reasonable steps to minimise losses to creditors, i.e. attempted to persuade fellow directors at board meetings, etc. to take remedial action with the business finances. Section 214 (4) is helpful in this regard. It states:

> For the purposes of subsections (2) and (3) the facts which a director of a company ought to know or ascertain, the conclusions which he ought to reach and the steps which he ought to take are those which would be known or ascertained or reached or taken, by a reasonably diligent person having both
>
> (a) the general knowledge, skill and experience that may reasonably be expected of a person carrying out the same functions as are carried out by that director in relation to the company, and
>
> (b) the general knowledge, skill and experience that that director has.

Point (a) is objective in that a minimum standard of knowledge, care, etc. is expected. However, point (b) is subjective since many considerations, e.g. the size of the company, whether the director concerned is qualified or not and other more general aspects of the case will be taken into account by the court.

The application of s. 214 is largely a matter of evidence and is geared towards fairness so far as the director is concerned. The court will weigh all the evidence and take into account current commercial practice. Obviously the general standing of the company's creditors in a case of a director's wrongful trading will be affected by any court order covering contribution from that director to the company assets. The decision in *Re Produce Marketing Consortium Ltd* (1989) gives a useful warning to directors in this matter.

The whole question of fraudulent and wrongful trading is thus crucial to a liquidator in the course of winding up a company in insolvent liquidation. Fraud – in whatever form – may be a criminal matter whenever committed but these two aspects of directors' delinquency come before the court during the course of winding up. Whether or not any action is taken against a delinquent director must in part depend on whether any substantial recovery is likely (aside from any question of fraud).

Remuneration of liquidators and trustees

Since the fees charged by a liquidator or trustee are a first call on the (unsecured) assets of the estate of the company or insolvent individual, the level of costs are clearly of direct interest to the creditors in each case.

The rules covering fees for both liquidators and trustees are similar (Insolvency Rules numbers 4.127 and 6.138) and details are set out below.

Basis of charges

The basis of charges is as follows:

● a percentage of the value of assets which are realised or distributed, or of the one value and the other in combination;

or

● by reference to the time properly given by the insolvency practitioner (as liquidator or trustee) and his staff.

Who decides the level of fees

There are two possible options here. Either the liquidation (or creditors') committee will determine the level of remuneration if a committee is formed (where the official receiver undertakes either of the two offices then his fees are determined in accordance with the scale laid down for the official receiver by general regulations) or, if no liquidation (or creditors') committee is formed, the fees may be set by a resolution of creditors. If no decision is taken by either body specified (as appropriate) or by the creditors then the official receiver's scale may be applied.

It should be mentioned that in the case of a members' voluntary liquidation the fees of the liquidator shall be fixed by the shareholders of the company being wound up since they are alone in having any interest in this transaction.

Conclusion

The complex rules of both statute and common law which apply to insolvency are constantly being reviewed and changed. Indeed, at the time of writing it is known that DTI initiatives are being examined and evaluated by many interested bodies and amendments to existing laws must be expected. It is hoped that the many rules are seen in summary as being fair and equitable to both creditors and insolvents alike.

Index